"Insightful, daring decisions a fulfilling life. Snyder does a to develop and use intuition for more empowered leadership. In the process he puts intuition smack in the center of the map, where it should have been all along."

—Brian Collins, CEO of COLLINS

"If you are looking for a fresh new approach that will help your company set a powerful direction and make a wiser decision that your people can get behind, and create a more alive and engaging place to work, look no further. *Decisive Intuition* is the blueprint for the empowered and innovative culture you've been waiting for."

—Dr. John Demartini, international bestselling author,
The Values Factor

DECISIVE INTUITION

INTUITION

USE YOUR GUT INSTINCTS TO MAKE
SMART BUSINESS DECISIONS

RICK SNYDER

CAREER
PRESS

This edition first published in 2019 by Career Press, an imprint of
Red Wheel/Weiser, LLC
With offices at:
65 Parker Street, Suite 7
Newburyport, MA 01950
www.redwheelweiser.com

ISBN: 978-1-63265-147-1

Library of Congress Cataloging-in-Publication
Data available upon request.

Cover design by Rob Johnson
Cover image by iStock.com
Interior photos/images by Frank Feinbork
Interior by Gina Schenck
Typeset in Minion Pro and Avenir Next Condensed

Printed in Canada
MAR
10 9 8 7 6 5 4 3 2 1

This book is dedicated to the individual divine spark inside us that we carry, often forget, and sometimes have to be reminded about daily. May we each continue to bring our deep listening and curiosity to this subtle whisper, our quiet confidant and reliable copilot that simply wants to guide us toward our greatest triumphs, fulfillment, and joy, no matter how much we kick and scream along the way.

CONTENTS

Introduction

1

Chapter 1

Intuition Demystified

13

Chapter 2

The Five Obstacles to Intuition

33

Chapter 3

You Don't Find Your Intuition; Your Intuition Finds You

61

Chapter 4

Slowing Down *Is* an Action Step

83

Chapter 5

Befriend Your Inner Critic

105

Chapter 6

Your Body Is Wiser than Your Mind

127

Chapter 7

Ask for Guidance

151

Chapter 8

Act on Your Inner Intelligence

171

Chapter 9
Make Your Company Culture Smarter
189

Notes
219

Acknowledgments
235

Index
239

About the Author
245

INTRODUCTION

When you reach the end of what you should know, you will be at the beginning of what you should sense.

—Kahlil Gibran

Have you ever had an experience during which you were given a clear, distinct message from inside? An inner guidance that wasn't coming from your head, but from a deeper place within? A sense of where you needed to move, whether that involved staying in or leaving a relationship, a new career path, or a new place to live? I'm not talking about your thoughts, but something even deeper. That was exactly what happened to me.

I felt called to the South of France to write this book while I was still living in Oregon. I'll never forget sitting in my room, looking out the window, and getting a familiar and clear message to move to France. I even looked down at my heart center where the inner voice came from and said, "But I don't even speak French!" Yet somewhere inside me, I realized that this was secondary to the larger calling that was whispering to me in that moment. I knew that it was time to shake things up for my next life adventure. I needed to follow the deep impulse inside of me. One that wouldn't go away. It didn't make sense to my rational mind, yet I learned to trust my inner guidance and knew that it was coming from a deeper well than the one my logical mind drank from.

I spent many years as a licensed therapist, life coach, business coach, and seeker, always looking for better ways to help people reach their potential, as I looked for the same myself. I immersed myself deeply in several paradigms and methodologies of personal growth, business development, and psychology, yet felt unsatisfied in teaching and leading other people's work. It was time to find my own creative expression. I knew that I needed to get away from everything familiar in order to have a new perspective. I scaled my business so I could operate it remotely, and I wasn't getting any younger. This was my best chance to make a leap into the unknown, guided by my inner GPS, and to live what I wanted to teach.

While working with business owners and managers throughout the past fifteen years in different capacities, I realized that there was a key element missing in the conversations about leadership development, company culture, and innovation. I didn't have the word for it then, but eventually realized there was an "invisible edge" that certain business owners and managers had that separated them from the rest. Some people embodied an ineffable quality that others naturally followed. The leaders who were comfortable enough with themselves to trust and develop their intuitive skills were the ones willing to take risks and disrupt the business landscape. They were on the leading edge of their lives, and their companies were benefitting. I knew that I needed to live this out in my own right.

It was time to integrate how business, psychology, and intuition fit together in the same conversation in order to help business men, women, and teams innovate to the next level. Business represents for me the grounded way that we transact value in terms of exchanging money for goods and services. Anything can become a business if we translate the value of what we are offering to an interested marketplace. Psychology is how we think about business and ourselves. It is how we "do" relationships, which is the essence of business. Psychology is at the root of strategy, how we change and adapt as leaders, study our markets, motivate our teams, learn how to communicate more effectively, and establish our overall perspective.

Intuition is our deeper intelligence that is able to read the room or the marketplace, make decisions from a wiser resource, and extract data faster than the conscious mind can analyze. Intuition is an entrepreneur's best friend. Psychology has finally become accepted in the business world after decades of suspicion and caution regarding the value of "soft skills" versus technical skills. Today, it is rare to find a business owner or manager who doesn't appreciate the advantages and impact of psychology in regards to understanding oneself, staff, and customers. With the advent of Daniel Goldman's book *Emotional Intelligence,*[1] qualities such as empathy, compassion, and self-awareness are now commonly accepted soft skills and values that need to be developed as much as, if not more than, harder technical skills. Emotional intelligence is understood more than ever as a necessary business principle in terms of staff engagement, healthy communication, and a thriving company culture.

And although the merging of business with psychology for more impactful results is evident, understanding the power of integrating intuition is still in its infancy. This is the missing link in making better decisions, guided by our innate intelligence that draws from our deeper subconscious mind and body. I see intuitive intelligence as a severely underdeveloped resource, and the *next wave of business evolution,* as we continue to unlock our untapped potential and utilize all of the data inside of us and around us for our best decision-making.

Intuition has gotten a bad rap. It's more often thought of as a touchy-feely, intangible skill, with a mix of superstition, New Age claptrap, and implicit bias, than as a true resource of a deeper intelligence and instinct inherent in each of us. In fact, author, research scientist, and *Harvard Business Review* contributor Andrew McAfee stated, "In the business world, decision-making based on intuition and gut feel should be driven out as ruthlessly as the Spanish Inquisition rooted out heretics. . . . Human experts are overconfident, inconsistent, and subject to a swarm of thoroughly documented biases, most of which they're not even aware of."[2]

Daniel Kahneman, a Nobel laureate in economics and author of *Thinking, Fast and Slow,* also warned of the biases of intuition and how our thinking can easily be influenced irrationally. He wrote that just because a thing feels right doesn't make it right, and, "Subjective confidence in a judgment is not a reasoned evaluation of the probability that this judgment is correct."[3] He pointed out that "people let their likes and dislikes determine their beliefs about the world."[4] He proposed that intuitive judgments are impulsive, neither clearly thought through nor critically examined. He encouraged the reader to combat overconfidence by basing beliefs not on subjective feelings but on critical thinking and logical reasoning. Kahneman effectively points out the multitude of ways that our perceptions can falsely influence our reality.

But the point of this book differs from those presented by Kahneman and McAfee. In this book, I propose that *intuition and critical thinking are not adversaries.* In fact, we make better decisions when we integrate intuition with critical thinking. Instead of seeing intuition and critical thinking as opposing forces and believing in the either-or, right brain versus left brain argument for which one should reign supreme, it's time for us to embrace intuition as a valuable source of information.

In this book I go one step further, arguing that with the advent of artificial intelligence, big data, and the Digital Age, intuition is needed now more than ever to balance humanity and emotional intelligence with vast swathes of data so that we can make good decisions. The future isn't a pure projection of the past. Data doesn't always anticipate anomalies or major shifts in culture, technology, the environment, and so forth. The inability of data to anticipate changes, coupled with the fact that institutions condition us *not* to trust intuition but instead focus on critical thinking and data, has caused an imbalance in business leadership, decision-making, and innovation. At a time when adaptive leadership is more important than ever, *intuition is the most important skill that we need to develop as leaders and as human beings.*

The title of this book, *Decisive Intuition,* speaks directly to the need for holding the tension between these two polarities. On one hand, leadership necessitates making decisions, taking risks, setting clear direction, and taking action. Executing a plan is critical for success. Intuition requires us to step back, slow down, and open up to the bigger picture as we take in all the data around us for a more holistic view. When we slow down, our intuition allows us to include more information and make wiser decisions. The successful disruptors and change agents are the ones who have learned how to integrate decisive action based on their intuitive intelligence.

It's time for intuition to be respected as a deeper source of intelligence that enhances our everyday decision-making. What if intuition were accessible to all of us? What if it could be learned, developed, and refined? And what if it could be used for practical business applications that combine the left and right sides of the brain? These applications could give real results, separating your company from the competition by enabling the members of your team to soar to new heights of creativity, outside-the-box thinking, and innovation.

Intuition is intrinsic to who we are. We shut ourselves off from a deeper wellspring of our intelligence and wisdom by ignoring the guidance and insight that intuition can provide. Companies need effective communication, decision-making, team building, and innovation to not only survive but thrive. In my experience as a business coach, a person who actively incorporates intuition into his or her leadership style achieves exactly that.

There's a reason that *intuition* and *intuitive leadership* are becoming some of the hottest buzzwords in business, as reflected in the top business magazines such as the *Harvard Business Review*, *Fast Company, Inc., Entrepreneur,* and *Forbes.* The word *intuition* is often used synonymously with *innovation* and *adaptability.* "I rely far more on gut instinct than researching huge amounts of statistics," said Richard Branson.[5]

In fact, trusting your gut instinct is a common trait reported by successful entrepreneurs such as Steve Jobs, Warren Buffett, and Oprah Winfrey. That belies the theories of statisticians and researchers who try to methodically plan and predict future behavior. According to Oprah, "Learning to trust your instincts, using your intuitive sense of what's best for you, is paramount for any lasting success. I've trusted the still, small voice of intuition my entire life. And the only time I've made mistakes is when I didn't listen."[6]

In an age when innovators are winning, business leaders and managers are encouraging their teams to think outside the box to get the greatest advantage. Companies such as Google, Nike, and Apple are investing in alternative practices such as mindfulness, meditation, and yoga to improve company culture and performance. These practices also assist staff in accessing their subconscious minds to discover the next hack or disruption in the industry.[7]

Understanding how to better access and apply intuition is likewise gaining traction in this highly competitive landscape. Mindfulness-based practices bring your full attention and awareness to the present moment through thoughts, feelings, bodily sensations, and the surrounding environment, and set the stage for accessing intuition. Mindfulness is great for mental health, relationships, and self-awareness, but it's the actionable ability of decisive intuition that sets it apart, which is most relevant in a business context. Mindfulness is what you do on the yoga mat. Intuition is what you do when you get up from the mat, making decisions that are in alignment with your gut sense and create change.

Building intuitive skills enables companies to anticipate the future. Decisions are made faster and patterns are recognized more quickly. Strategy and direction are forged more clearly yet can adapt to new data. Intuitive thinking is how businesses can stay agile in today's ever-changing environment and marketplace. Once intuitive decision-making is developed and practiced, a team doesn't need twenty-seven meetings to come to agreement. As neuroscience continues to advance, we are seeing practical evidence of how intuition affects every aspect of a business. An article entitled "Intuition in Organizations" states, "In a range of studies, intuitive judgment has been found to be associated positively not only with the quality and speed of decisions, but also the financial and non-financial performance of the wider organization."[8]

Intuition enables us to read, in real time, what's happening, which gives us more choices for how to respond. And the best part is that it's not mystical but rather a skill set that each of us can learn to cultivate. And like any skill or characteristic, it takes work to develop. The ones who are integrating their intuitive nature with their business decisions are leading. And those around them are taking note.

This book presents three foundational principles that are changing the landscape of business and our human potential:

1. **Intuition is connected to a deeper intelligence inside all of us that enriches our lives personally, professionally, and creatively.** The conscious, rational mind is limited. When we open ourselves to the intelligence in our bodies and our non-conscious mind, the well we draw from gains more depth and breadth to inform us.

2. **Intuition can be learned, developed, and refined, like any skill or characteristic.** But we have to work at it. The ability to recognize intuitive patterns, nuances, and subtlety increases through exposure, listening, and practice.

3. **Intuition applied to business by integrating inner knowing with logic and critical thinking creates a distinct advantage.** Innovators are the winners in today's business environment. Adopters of intuition are engaged and passionate, because they're innovating beyond their competition and cocreating a purposeful, switched-on place to work. They're having fun while succeeding!

Intuition plays by different rules and can threaten those who rely primarily on empirical evidence, such as data and analytics, when making critical decisions. Yet as we deepen our relationship with inner knowing, we build confidence and open up creativity and possibility. We learn to trust ourselves, along with the signs and signals that our internal system is asking us to pay attention to. People are a company's greatest asset, and personal development is no longer just an option for those who are ready to step outside the conventional box and achieve great things. Yet the question that each business leader struggles to answer is: *How* do you train and develop intuitive skills in a team to achieve the greatest result for the business?

This book is for business leaders and managers who want answers to this question and are ready to improve their company culture. It's also for employees who want to develop their potential in how they contribute each day. It's for anyone who sees value in striking the right balance between having a clear direction based on research and data and including the subtlest sensory input to make the most informed decisive intuition possible. In *Decisive Intuition,* I will lead you through the following six-step process, which taps into your intuitive intelligence to improve decision-making, leadership, and innovation.

1. **Become more receptive.** The first step for getting in touch with your intuitive nature is all about learning how to be receptive to your environment and beginning to open your senses to the conversation that's already happening around you and inside of you.

2. **Slow down.** Intuition can only be found in the present moment. When you slow down your thoughts and turn away from outside distraction, you begin to notice the quiet voice of your intuition that's speaking to you right now.

3. **Separate from your inner critic.** Once you slow down, you'll often hear the voice of your inner critic chime in and get louder, which distracts you from the voice of your intuition. Learning how to separate the voice of your critic from the voice of your intuition is paramount.

4. **Listen to your body.** After you distill the voice of your intuition, you can then drop in deeper to listen to what your inner signals and cues are telling you throughout your body and nonconscious mind.

5. **Ask for guidance.** Now that you have decoded your intuitive language, you can depend on the relationship with your inner guidance system by asking a question that needs addressing in the business, and actually get a response!

6. **Act on your inner intelligence.** Lastly, you'll discover how to take action based on your essential wisdom and nature. This is where impactful change happens as you are connected to a deeper purpose and serving, not only yourself in a deeper way, but those around you. Bringing your feelings into action is the birthplace of true creativity, possibility, and innovation.

We'll explore the specific business applications and profound results for each of these steps. We'll also shed new light on what gets in the way of your intuition so that you can begin to overcome some of these obstacles and gain more access to your natural intelligence. There's even a chapter dedicated to differentiating the voice of your inner critic from the voice of your intuition, which is one of the biggest hurdles in learning to listen to and trust your inner knowing.

This practical guide includes exercises that you and your team can implement to harness intuition and grow the most underdeveloped skill set in today's business culture. You'll read real stories from my years as a business coach helping companies leverage intuitive practices to make sound decisions about personnel, hold effective meetings, and think strategically. You'll hear from business leaders and managers from South Africa to Silicon Valley who have successfully incorporated intuition into their sales strategy, decision-making, and company cultures. We'll explore the latest research into neurobiology and flow states, and how that research supports the call for the further development of intuition. You'll also hear about the painful consequences experienced by business leaders who didn't listen to what their inner sense was telling them—the consequences that made them declare, "Never again!"

It's time to double down on the creativity and ingenuity of human beings. This book connects the dots on how to ignite the collective wisdom of the members of your team into your company culture, to improve communication, execution, and results. You'll see how to apply intuition to every corner of your business, including product development, anticipating the market, hiring and personnel decisions, investment pitching, negotiation, the overall strategy for growth, cash forecasting, and so much more.

Decisive Intuition takes us beyond the old narrative of the false opposites of right brain versus left brain, hard science vs. soft science, and inner wisdom versus data and analytics. It moves the conversation toward an integration of our inner knowing and guidance with critical thinking and analytics to give us the best chance to succeed in business (and in life). I am excited to share this exploration with you and to hear what you discover about yourself and how your work life transforms as a result.

INTUITION DEMYSTIFIED

It is through science that we prove, but through intuition that we discover.

—Henri Poincare

Nelia Joubert was sweating under her sheets, but she didn't know exactly why.[1] Her company had just landed a dream gig: a huge wedding for the nephew of South Africa's president, Jacob Zuma. Things were in motion, seemingly going great, and yet she was tossing and turning all night and couldn't shake the feeling that something felt "off."

Nelia and her business partner, Zane Carim, joined forces a couple of years earlier to form White Rabbit Productions, an event production and management company in Johannesburg, South Africa. Their company produces a wide range of events, including awards shows, corporate events, custom parties, and weddings in South Africa and beyond. They were elated when one of their suppliers referred them to Zuma's representatives to help stage one of the most high-profile weddings in the country.

All hands were on deck as they worked around the clock to put together all of the details for the initial proposal. With a multi-million-dollar budget, they planned for more than 2,000 guests. The event was also going to be covered by the major media networks.

This event was the opportunity that Nelia and Zane had been dreaming of for their budding company—the opportunity to show the country and the world the White Rabbit way. In addition to providing great profit and making the company financially stable for the near future, it would enable them to showcase their unique flare for creativity, deliver a memorable experience for the wedding party and international guests, and make a splash in the industry. They were thrilled.

After initial talks with Zuma's representatives, they were tasked with handling the entire event's infrastructure. There were so many moving parts in coordinating the wedding, including celebrations in Swaziland and South Africa, and dealing with the multitude of vendors and suppliers. Everything was going smoothly, but Nelia couldn't shake the feeling in the pit of her stomach that something was off.

She decided to ignore the feeling because she and Zane were flying to Swaziland that afternoon to see the venue and put finishing touches on the final proposal so that they could move closer to the contract. She didn't want to share her doubts and fears with Zane and come off as a downer, especially since she had nothing concrete to point to. She convinced herself that she was just anxious and her concerns would be resolved after meeting with Zuma's representatives to gather information about the logistics.

Upon arrival, Nelia and Zane agreed that they were impressed by the natural beauty of the venue and had favorable initial impressions of everyone they met. Zuma's representatives must have been equally impressed because they told Nelia and Zane to come back with a final budget and they would make it happen. The project was going to be a three-week setup with no expense spared. White Rabbit had never thrown a party for someone with such deep pockets. Nelia was caught up in the moment. Her creative juices were flowing as she thought about what the White Rabbit team could accomplish. The artist in her was doing cartwheels. Hands were shaken and verbal agreements made.

They had no time to waste. As soon as they returned to Johannesburg, they paid deposits to the suppliers and set the wheels in motion. As a young business, White Rabbit didn't have a lot of money to front, but Nelia and Zane knew that this wasn't the time to hesitate. All of their experience culminated in that moment. They were ready.

Nelia was buzzing. This was the greatest opportunity of her life. It was what she and Zane had always wanted. But something inside her was still telling her to stop. And as much as she tried to push that nagging feeling down, it wouldn't go away. She had a sense that the event wasn't going to happen. Something wasn't right. Yet she had no direct evidence to support her intuition. She wanted to share her feeling with Zane, but she hesitated.

What would her business partner say? Would he chalk it up to pressure from such a big opportunity getting to her? Would he give any credence to her feeling? She wondered whether she might be second-guessing herself.

After another sleepless night of being tormented by her internal radar, Nelia knew that Zane wouldn't take her feeling seriously unless she took it seriously first. She remembered the time they hired a new project manager. Although his resume seemed perfect, she knew he wasn't the right fit. Yet, she let the urgency of the moment override her inner knowing. Soon enough, he was volatile with staff and rude to clients, and eventually stormed off the job. She now thought of several instances, such as when she and Zane chose the wrong accountant or promised a too-ambitious deadline, when she had an inner sense that turned out to be dead-on.

In the next few days, they received mixed signals. Some of Zuma's representatives said they would sign and pay money now, but others said they would sign and pay later. Too many different stories of the vision for the wedding and how it was going to be financed were floating around. There was a growing feeling of chaos smoothed over with smiles and conversation.

White Rabbit was on the verge of paying another round of deposits to suppliers and vendors. Nelia was feeling increasingly uneasy about the situation, and she knew she had to say something. Finally, she pulled Zane aside and said, "I don't feel comfortable with this. I've had this growing sense in my belly, for weeks now, that something just isn't right, that this event won't happen, and we'll put our business in jeopardy if we keep fronting more money for deposits. I know what's at stake here. I want this more than anything, but this feeling won't go away. In fact, it keeps getting stronger."

Zane was startled at first. And then he became angry. They had a heated exchange. Although Zane agreed that Zuma's representatives had waffled in their commitments, he said that he and Nelia should give them the benefit of a doubt. This project was the break they'd been looking for. He chalked up her fears to a case of cold feet.

But Nelia took a stand. She dug in deeper to what she had been feeling. She had nothing to lose in sharing her truth, even in the face of someone who didn't have the same intuitive sense. Although Zane's points were logical, she didn't budge.

Finally, Zane seemed to feel—or at least appreciate—her inner conviction. After some more back and forth, something shifted in the argument and Zane pivoted. He took a deep breath, looked at her, and said, "Hey, you've been right in the past. So, if you're feeling that strongly about it, let's walk away from it." He stood by Nelia's call.

From the outside looking in, walking away was business suicide. Yet Nelia and Zane were honoring something deeper. Zane was trusting Nelia's intuition more than the short-term win, as difficult as that decision was for him.

On the eve of signing the contract and paying additional deposits, Nelia and Zane made the final decision to pull out of the project. The following week, the scandal came out. President Zuma had been embezzling money from the government. Some of the wedding festivities were expected to take place at Zuma's residence, which had been funded by stolen money.

As soon as the story went viral, the wedding was canceled. It was a big blow to all involved, with four major companies supporting various aspects of the event. All of them suffered big losses. Nelia told me that one of the other companies had canceled all of its other events to do the wedding and then lost everything.

Although White Rabbit lost the deposits it had paid to secure its suppliers for those dates, the company's losses would have been far greater if Zane hadn't listened to Nelia's intuition. White Rabbit would have spent a lot more money and time and then not gotten paid. On top of that, the company would have gotten a tremendous amount of negative press. The positive exposure Nelia and Zane hoped for would have turned into a PR nightmare since the wedding would have been partially financed by stolen money. Acting on Nelia's intuition saved White Rabbit.

Nelia risked taking a stand. She chose to stay true to herself, even in the face of her desire to have a big-name company with abundant cash flow, new opportunities, and a stellar reputation. Not only had they dodged a bullet, but she set the tone for White Rabbit's management to make future decisions from this internal place of integrity.

Nelia never questioned her intuition again. Her decision-making became more finely tuned. Her communication became even more authentic and straightforward in recruiting, projects, and determining which clients to take on. She realized that it all was connected. If she wasn't listening to her intuition, she wasn't taking care of herself, her company, or her clients. After the Zuma experience, clients trusted Nelia even more. People can feel when others truly trust and listen, even if they don't have the words to explain that feeling in the moment.

As Nelia's story illustrates, listening to our inner guidance as business leaders, decision-makers, and as people is no longer an option in business today. Overriding our inner knowing with the promise of more revenues, profit, market share, and recognition is so easy. Yet, we pay a steep price if those are the only metrics we pay attention to. Quick wins don't hold their weight in the long run if we're not aligned with an inner compass for decision-making. However, many of us are not well practiced in listening to and trusting inner guidance. Many of us don't even know it's on the menu.

Remember when you knew that a new hire or strategy was a bad idea but you ignored that feeling? Or when you knew your partner was cheating but you didn't listen to your gut? Remember how frustrated you were with yourself afterward? I personally feel such a sense of betrayal when I ignore my intuition. That feeling has awakened me to the gift and value of what happens when we lead our businesses and live our lives in tune with our intuition.

So, what exactly is intuition? And where does it come from? The word *intuition* comes from the Latin root *intueri*, which translates to "look upon," "contemplate," or "to look within." Throughout the centuries, intuition has become synonymous with a spiritual insight or an instinctive feeling rather than conscious thought or logical reasoning. Since ancient Greek times, intuition has been seen as coming from a source other than the rational mind. Intuition is often defined as the ability to understand something immediately without the need for conscious reasoning. In this book, I'll use a more applicable definition: an embodied knowing that comes from listening to what wants to happen next. This " knowing" is one that doesn't just come from our conscious mind, but from all of our senses, including what we pick up from our nonconscious mind. There's a critical element of being receptive. By listening to what wants to happen, you allow the surrounding data to inform you on what action steps need to be executed. I'll use various terms throughout the book that are synonymous and replaceable with the word *intuition,* such as "inner guidance," "inner compass," "inner GPS," "gut sense," "inner radar," "true north," and "inner navigational system."

This book is about cultivating the oldest relationship and the oldest source of wisdom we have: ourselves. It's about moving the

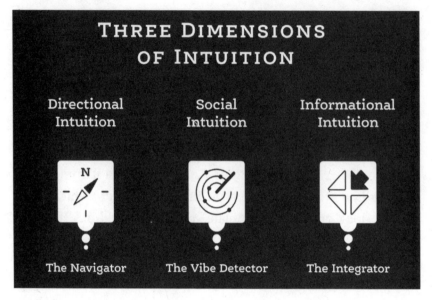

THREE DIMENSIONS OF INTUITION

Directional Intuition — The Navigator

Social Intuition — The Vibe Detector

Informational Intuition — The Integrator

Figure 1.

conversation from the mystical to the practical. It is about reconnecting with a deeper resource of innate intelligence to achieve more effective communication, decision-making, leadership, and innovation.

By combining in-depth research, countless interviews with business leaders around the world, and case studies from my role as a business coach and business owner, I categorized intuition into three dimensions that people exemplify to varying degrees. These three dimensions, *directional, social,* and *informational,* have a tremedous impact on business (see Figure 1).

Directional Intuition: "The Navigator"

The directional dimension of intuition is your center point that orients you with your day-to-day business decisions, which align with your life's direction and purpose. It is your personal connection to your inner guidance or innate wisdom. It connects you with the inner you in the most intimate way. Depending on your lens or belief system, directional intuition is commonly described as guidance from your higher self, soul, divine nature, subconscious mind, the environment, the field, or the grand order of things. The idea is that you have an intuitive guidance system embedded deeply in your being that is connected to something greater than your conscious mind, and it picks up on information all around you, all the time. Even when you sleep! It is the source of your inner compass. And to connect with this guidance system, you need to be receptive to listening to these frequencies, which are quite different from everyday thoughts. Some people see directional intuition as the spiritual or mystical access point that connects to a deeper, universal intelligence beyond the egoic mind-personality, yet is still centrally connected to it.

On a practical level, it's your "navigator," which helps you maneuver the daily challenges and opportunities in your business and in life. Directional intuition orients you to the "true north" in your business decisions and guides you toward the next evolutionary steps in your life's journey, even if your conscious mind has no clue what's happening. Have you ever felt that a job or a relationship was past its expiration date or wasn't right in the first place but couldn't figure out why? Maybe everything looked great on paper, but something told you that it was time for your next adventure. Have you ever moved somewhere or followed a calling that didn't make sense to you at the time?

I interviewed Marc David, the founder of The Institute for the Psychology of Eating and the author of the bestselling books

Nourishing Wisdom: A Mind-Body Approach to Nutrition and Well-Being and *The Slow Down Diet: Eating for Pleasure, Energy, and Weight Loss.* He shared how the moments of listening to his directional intuition and taking action helped him pioneer the key business manifestations for his life.

> *I don't know that I have a more important navigational system than my intuition. At the end of the day, when I look at how I get from point A to point B in my life, how I make big decisions, how I arrive at where I'm going to live, what college I'm going to go to, what grad school I'm going to go to, what woman I'm going to date, to me, intuition always factors in in a big way—if not in a really big way. I don't think I can operate without it. I wouldn't even know how to do that. I would feel uncomfortably naked if I didn't have it.*
>
> *Intuition is this voice that comes through that somehow doesn't usually sound like the "me, me, me, me, me." It has a different quality to it. It has a smarter quality to it. It has a more timeless quality to it. It has a more relaxed quality to it. It ain't worried. When intuition is speaking, it's a clear bell and it's very confident.[2]*

Social Intuition: "The Vibe Detector"

Once you find the origin point of your inner guidance and directional intuition, you can now extend beyond yourself to feel and sense other people. The social dimension of intuition is based on one's ability to read the energies and emotions—the vibe—among people in a room or the room itself. It is your "vibe detector." Social intuition is related to animal instinct in navigating safety, protection, and connection. Although we may not be consciously aware of doing it, we pick up on nonverbal communication cues, congruence, and dissonance all of the time.

For example, imagine you're in a meeting with new people. Right away, you don't trust the guy sitting to your left. Everything that he says sounds like a lie. There's something about him that you just don't trust, however, you immediately trust the woman sitting to your right. She seems open and friendly. You may or may not be accurate in either case. Yet, like all creatures, we rely on these instincts. And these instincts are animal instincts. Social intuition feels very neurological and primordial. It's subtle. Animals use it all the time. When two of us meet, we sense each other, we size each other up, and sniff each other out. We growl on the inside, hope to win the other's attention and approval, or simply feel neutral about the other.

When I waited tables, one of the first things I did was read the needs of the people at each table so that I could provide the type of service that would best suit them. The salespeople out there know what I'm talking about. On one hand, some tables want little to no interaction with a server. Perhaps they're on a romantic night out or in the middle of a serious conversation and don't want to be interrupted.

On the other hand, the people at another table might be bored with one another and see going out as their big entertainment for the week. In that case, they want an engaging, entertaining experience from the server. Or maybe a table is filled with people who don't know one another well or who are socially awkward. A good server needs to be able to track the energies and nonverbal cues from the people at the table so that he or she can facilitate the customer experience.

Social intuition has huge implications in the business world. An executive or manager needs to be able to sense when a meeting, sales presentation, or investment pitch is falling flat and what needs to happen next to bring more engagement and vitality to the conversation. Social intuition is the key to sales, developing relationships, and building trust. The ability to intuit the needs of a customer at every stage of the client experience is an incredible edge over your competition. Developing this dimension of intuition also increases engagement on your team because you are able to track social dynamics and nonverbal communication, which help in reading complex interactions with individuals and groups.

Informational Intuition: "The Integrator"

The informational dimension of intuition is an awareness that extends even further out between you and other people, and encompasses the whole environment. It is the ability to synthesize and integrate large amounts of data and decode information rapidly for analysis, pattern recognition, and decision-making in your surroundings. Those who possess this gift have an innate ability to quickly recognize patterns and analyze information and experiences—including those stored in the subconscious mind. Leading financial investors, data scientists, day traders, researchers, and engineers often excel at this ability.

In *Blink,* Malcolm Gladwell described informational intuition as "the part of our brain that leaps to conclusions . . . called the adaptive unconscious."[3] In fact, one of the main points of Gladwell's book is that decisions made quickly can be as good as decisions based on extensive research and contemplation. He called this superpower "thin-slicing": "the ability of our unconscious to find patterns in situations and behavior based on very narrow slices of experience."[4] An example that he gives recounts how researcher John Gottman and his team at the University of Washington could determine with 90 percent accuracy if a couple will still be married in fifteen years' time—by observing their interaction for just fifteen minutes. They later discovered that if they observed only three minutes of a couple talking they could predict who would make it and who wouldn't, with still-impressive accuracy.

Daniel Caruana of Danrae Waterproofing, a multimillion-dollar business in Sydney, Australia, shared some of the secrets to his success using informational intuition:

With numbers, I'm able to intuitively see if there's something wrong. What I'll do is call those around me to give me their feedback, and I'll either dismiss it or choose that advice. With our weekly financial report, I can see intuitively when there are issues there. I have a feel for trends and how things should be. I'll pause and take a deeper look if something looks off. Then I'll call upon our CFO and accountants to discuss this. Recently, we had a resourcing issue and realized billable hours were going down. Liquidity and profitability as well. The numbers were also reflecting another observation: The attitude and motivation of staff were declining. So, it's a mix of tangible and intangibles that I have to feel through. All of this was a reflection that something had to change. And my relationship with our numbers has helped us navigate our challenges over the years.[5]

Integrate Directional, Social, and Informational Intuition

What does it look like to combine all three dimensions of intuition in decision-making? Imagine you are in the middle of a business deal with another party. The first step is to check in with your directional intuition and let your inner compass orient you. Can you trust the facts and figures that are being presented? Do you feel open and willing to work things through, or are you feeling tight and cautious inside? Does something not seem right, even if you don't know what it is? Sometimes the deal looks great; you have a glimmer in your eye as you know you are over charging the other party and are going to make an incredible profit. You might find yourself getting overly excited and greedy, but you are unbalanced. From here, your position is over extended from your center point, and this will affect your perspective and negotiations. I've seen businesspeople knowingly take advantage of others, and eventually this comes out and impacts future negotiations.

On the other end, are you not clear about your true value? Are you giving away too much? If this is the case, you are collapsing from your center point and inviting the other party to take advantage of you. Either way, something is not balanced in the business deal. Something is off. You have to be connected with your own core first. Otherwise, you will play out dramas based on projections of who you think the other stakeholders are as well as their intentions, versus coming from a clear awareness of what's really happening. Your inner compass is where you start negotiating from.

Once your directional intuition is finely tuned to your own orientation, you can activate your social intuition and sense what's happening in the room with the other players. What do you feel and notice when you are across the table? Are they trustworthy? Is there a resonance with the other negotiators? Or do you feel something off with the other stakeholders? This is where emotional intelligence, body language, and social dynamics are so incredibly important in business. Professional poker players constantly utilize social intuition to discern who they are playing with.

Lastly, you can now extend beyond the others in the room and tune in to the whole environment, as your informational intuition is now ignited. What is the gestalt of the whole space around the negotiations? Is the timing right? Does it feel like you or the other parties are forcing something, or is it naturally clicking into place? This is where you look at all the data, numbers, and figures and keep feeling for resonance. You might feel positive about the deal and the other players involved, yet something still doesn't feel right. This is where you rely on your own experience and explore all of the variables involved. Perhaps you didn't consider the additional escrow cost or if there's an alternative way to get the products shipped from China. Perhaps one stakeholder is taking a 20 percent cut that is out of proportion from what they are putting into the deal. You might not know what it is, but trust your intuition until the data starts to make sense.

On a deeper level, we are all looking for a fair and equitable exchange, and all parties will know when they come to this if they are operating from their intuitive intelligence. To summarize, you start with locating your own reference point; then you make sure everyone in the room is on the same page and resonant with the deal; and lastly, you do your due diligence and ensure all moving parts are in sync to move forward.

In other words, the three dimensions of intuition are about a deep, intimate connection with yourself, others, and your environment. The common factor is the ability to access a deeper source of intelligence outside your conscious mind and use it to inform your next steps. Intuition is about your relationship with yourself first and then about your relationships with others and the environment at large. It's about learning your own rhythms and signals for when something feels off or right on the money. Learning to trust your intuition is the greatest gift you can give yourself. It makes the difference in business decisions and it enables you to have a purposeful, fulfilling life. And it just feels good to trust yourself once you've cultivated a relationship with your intuition.

In addition to businesses, the military is recognizing the integration of intuition as a competitive edge. In 2014, the Office of Naval Research embarked on a four-year, $3.85 million-dollar research project to explore intuition and what they call "Spidey sense" for sailors and Marines.[6] The research includes ways to explore intuitive decision-making that can result in the ability to make better decisions in the field, which could save lives. "If we can characterize this intuitive decision-making process and model it, then the hope is to accelerate the acquisition of these skills," says Lieutenant Commander Brent Olde.[7]

In fact, in Mark Divine's book, *The Way of the SEAL: Think Like an Elite Warrior to Lead and Succeed,* he discusses the role of intuition for an elite warrior. Mark drew on his experience as a Navy SEAL commander: "Most of your creativity and some of your best ideas will come from the hidden inner mind of your subconscious. Once you learn to harness this powerful intelligence, you will break through to new levels of awareness and accomplishments."[8]

Divine poignantly states, "Though many business people might scoff at what some consider 'hocus pocus' (or other choice terms), the modern warrior fields are regaining interest in the study and development of intuition."[9] If the elite warriors of the military are utilizing and incorporating intuition as a strategic and tactical advantage, you can bet it has merit and applications in other competitive fields, such as business.

The challenge is that as we are increasingly inundated by digital technology, it is easier than ever to be disconnected from our inner guidance systems. In fact, a 2011 University of Southern California study revealed that, on average, we process a daily volume of information equivalent to more than 174 newspapers, which is five times more than twenty years earlier.[10] Putting down the electronics and making the time and space to connect with inner wisdom is more difficult than ever. So, how can we embrace technology without losing connection to ourselves?

In this book, we'll explore one of the chief obstacles of cultivating intuition: our tendency to stay in the comfort zone of our minds and outside stimuli, rather than daring to venture into our bodies where we feel things. Yet life begins at the edge of the comfort zone. We feel more alive when we include all of our experiences rather than being stuck in our own heads. This book is a wake-up call to stop getting sucked into a passive way of being. I'm passionate about helping men and women live engaged, dynamic, courageous lives. Living those lives is a struggle now more than ever, with so many forms of entertainment fighting for our attention. Listening proactively to our inner guidance systems is the missing step in leadership, decision-making, innovation, and the powerful conversations that bring reward and purpose to our lives.

Intuition comes in many forms. Our inner compasses have unique languages, from feelings and sound to dreams and imagery. In this book, I propose that however your intuition communicates with you, it's always connected to a feeling and a deep sense of knowing that is distinct from your logical mind and from your fear responses, emotional impulses, and implicit bias. For example, you may be repulsed by, drawn to, or seduced by something, but your response may be coming from something other than intuition. We'll examine all of these forms of intuition in the real-life experiences of businesspeople and in practical exercises. The most important point is that you should get curious about the way *you* receive information and how *your* intuitive center operates.

To isolate intuition as a skill set that we can build, we make a distinction between *intuition* and *instinct*. Although there is overlap between the two (because they inform each other), for purposes of this conversation, *instinct* is centered on our hardwired response to survival and safety. Our basic instinct is laden with the genetic coding to survive, procreate, save a child from drowning without regard to our own safety, and so forth. A cat chasing a mouse is acting from instinct that is hardwired in its DNA. Social intuition overlaps with instinct to some degree, but focuses more on excelling at interpersonal relationships by recognizing nonverbal communication, social dynamics, and needs and wants of individuals and markets. It also focuses on intuiting the emotional and energetic needs and the concerns of others. Instinct focuses entirely on survival.

We are also delineating intuition from mindfulness-based practices. Mindfulness is often described as the moment-to-moment awareness of thoughts, feelings, bodily sensations, and the surrounding environment. Mindfulness is great for mental health, relationships, and self-awareness, and sets the stage for accessing intuition. Yet they are very distinct. It's the actionable ability of intuitive practices that sets it apart, which is most relevant in a business context. Mindfulness is what you do on the mat. Intuition is what you do when you get up from the mat, make decisions that are in alignment with your gut instinct, and create change.

Listening to and trusting intuition and then taking action based on intuition seems edgy. We may experience fear along with new insights and possibilities as we're confronted with what it means to really listen to our deep truth. What choices, losses, fears, and uncertainty await? Breaking away from routine, spreadsheets, and groupthink in decision-making is a new ball game. That will be scary at times, but ultimately it will be successful, meaningful, and keep you feeling alive and relevant in your career. If you don't listen to your intuition, you'll feel empty inside even if you're "successful."

The first way you can learn about intuition is to explore what gets in the way.

Let's begin the journey within.

Conclusion

Intuition is our innate intelligence and is distinct from instinct, insight, mindfulness, and something mystical. It is not at odds with data and analytics because it is time to take the best of our critical, rational mind and our deeper subconscious processing. When it comes to decision-making, intuition can be viewed as another critical stream of data that we should include in our conversations for a more holistic and well-rounded view. It's inherently woven into the fabric of our being on the deepest levels, so it is difficult to isolate, let alone notice. Most importantly, it's a skillset that we can develop and harness to use in business and in life to make the best choices possible that are in alignment with our own purpose and the environment at large.

The Five Obstacles to Intuition

Don't let the noise of other's opinion drown your own inner voice. Everything else is secondary.

—Steve Jobs

Daniel Caruana[1] sat in the boardroom of Danrae Waterproofing, a water damage repair and waterproofing company based in Sydney, shaking his head in disbelief. The director of sales was reading off last month's sales report, followed painfully by the financials. Daniel had served as general manager for several years and knew the business, but it was not his show. It was his father's. The leadership team was collectively pulling their hair out. Sales were drying up and they were dipping into credit to keep the business floating, with no easy solution in sight.

Daniel knew what he had to do. Ron Caruana, Daniel's father, founded and grew the company effectively. But Ron was not modernizing the systems, reporting, sales, and overall leadership of the business. As what happens so often in business, no one was confronting this underlying issue directly. Ron had grown comfortable with a winning formula that had worked for a couple of decades: focus on great relationships with customers and vendors, and the rest will sort itself out. But the business needed a different kind of leadership if it was going to remain a front-runner in the industry, let alone survive.

Daniel knew someone had to step into the CEO role to lead the company to its next destination, and he knew he was that person. Although he successfully built trust with his inner guidance, he was still fearful to take action. Right on cue, the lump in his throat prevented him from speaking up that morning.

Ron wasn't ready to hand over the business that he had founded. And although he knew what needed to happen, Daniel faced a cascade of doubts as to whether his father would let go of control, whether staff would take his leadership seriously, and whether he had what it took to lead the company successfully. The risks were steep. His parents' retirement was also tied up in the company's success, because they had invested so much personal money into running the business.

Not taking action was an action step. And the consequences mounted all around. On-site supervision of the crews wasn't happening on a regular basis, mistakes were being made in the field more regularly, they had no marketing plan or understanding of how to leverage social media for new clients, and making payroll was proving more difficult each month.

Daniel's intuition said, "You're letting this happen." As much as he had learned to trust his gut when it came to financial forecasting, hiring, and getting a read on the company culture, he was more conflicted than ever about taking action on his gut feeling.

His mind, and more specifically, his inner critic, said things like, "Well, I really shouldn't be the one to fill those shoes. I'm not really qualified. I shouldn't be in charge of my parents, who founded the business. This is not how it should work." Daniel was fighting years of conditioning to defer to authority. Not only was his father the founder and CEO, his mother served as CFO. Yet, when he dropped all the mental chatter and listened to that deeper place inside, he knew the old narrative didn't hold up to the stronger feeling of needing to take charge.

At this time, Daniel and Ron contracted with me for business coaching. I quickly identified the power dynamics and the conversation that needed to happen. I also sensed that Daniel needed some time to build up his confidence to be the leader his company needed, and to take the reins from Ron. Daniel admits that he needed a little push from those around him in order to step up. He asked one of his best mates, "How do I be a good leader?" And his friend replied, "You just be one." Something about that reflection really sunk in. After a few more sessions focused on role-plays and strengthening his resolve, Daniel realized he couldn't wait for the outside world to confirm what he felt. It was up to him to take action and stand for his convictions.

In our meetings, Ron worked on his fears regarding delegation and empowering others to lead. By holding onto the power, he didn't see how he was getting in his own way from what he ultimately wanted: freedom. The more I helped Ron get to the bottom of his fears and stay connected to the bigger picture for his life, the more he was able to surrender control responsibly.

One morning, Daniel sat across from Ron and found his authority. "Dad, I know what the problem is. For Danrae to grow,

I need to take over the leadership of this company. And I need your support for this to happen." Ron knew that Daniel was very capable and had more of a read on today's marketing and system-ization, as well as the passion and drive that it would take to lead Danrae to new horizons. It took a lot of trust to step down. After some initial objections, Ron listened to his own gut and finally got to a place where he was willing to give this a chance. He wanted to see his son and the business succeed. Deep down, he knew this was the best way forward. He was impressed by the strength he felt from his son across the table.

Two things happened that helped Ron let go and trust: First, they started to see results within months of the transition. New sales started to come in as it became more clear who their target customer was. They updated trainings for their teams and improved communication systems with customers, which led to more referrals. Second, Daniel continued to believe in his ability to lead the company toward profitability and success. He tuned out the inner critic and all of its doubts and fears, and kept listening to the deeper voice within—the one that told him he was on track. The more that he lived from this new reference point, the more the old voices and stories began to fall away. This transformation within Daniel was palpable to those around him.

At the end of 2017, Danrae had its best financial year ever. Their revenues tripled, they had healthy cash reserves, their company grew an additional 30 percent, and they moved into an up-graded headquarters as they continue to expand their operations beyond the Sydney metropolitan area. They are now on track to become a $25 million-dollar company. Daniel's ability to listen to his intuitive guidance and take action accordingly was what made the difference. He learned to trust his inner compass in leading his company with undeniable results through hiring decisions, financial strategy, new innovative services, and expanded marketplaces.

As Daniel's story indicates, intuition serves us in two different ways: We are able to increase our capacity to read what's happening in our immediate environment, and we can better anticipate the future. Yet, if we are not trained to be more still and present to what's happening in the moment, we will undoubtedly miss the rich signs and indicators that are waiting for our attention. In today's fast-paced and increasingly complex world, it is more difficult than ever to slow down and tune into what we are sensing and feeling on the inside.

Discovering the voice of your intuition is about returning to your natural state. It's a pivotal channel through which you receive information. Whether you get the sense that you are being ripped off by a salesperson, that you knew that you should have made a left instead of going straight (no matter what Google Maps said), that a certain job is not the right fit for you, or that this is the person you want to live your life with, the inner conversation is happening constantly. We have all been conditioned to tune-out, doubt, or override this inner resource. Most of us have never consciously created a relationship with our intuition, so it seems more foreign to us than our daily thoughts or other people's strong opinions that we internalize.

Many of us didn't get permission or support to discover a relationship with our inner voice and inner authority as we were busy downloading the perspectives and opinions of those around us. Often in family and school settings, we were taught what behaviors and attitudes were acceptable and which ones were not. Because the need to belong to a group was and continues to be so power-ful, it's easy to discount our own inner intelligence, especially if it goes against the rules or norms of those around us. There's a huge fear component in trusting our gut: What if we get kicked out of the group? What if we are wrong? If we rely solely on metrics and data sets for decision-making, at least we can blame bad data if we make mistakes! There's more at stake in taking full ownership of our decision-making power.

Three progressions prevent us from living from our intuitive center on a daily basis: We are challenged to listen to our intuition in the first place; we are challenged to trust our intuition when we get a message; or we are challenged to take action on what we feel. This chapter explores how we block our own intuitive nature, and thus our self-authority and empowerment.

Although there are many different ways that we can examine the obstacles to intuitive feeling, I have found it most helpful to group the "obstacles" of intuition into five distinct categories: the rational mind, doubt, busyness, fear, and the ego. Each of these runs interference on our ability to listen to, trust, and act from our deeper nature. In being able to identify these common roadblocks, we have a better chance of eliminating the most common distrac-tions and noise that we face, so that we can develop a relationship with our inner guidance for greater impact and self-fulfillment.

Obstacle 1: The Rational Mind

Over reliance on our rational, conscious mind is one of the great-est obstacles to accessing intuition. Our rational mind is based in the frontal cortex, which is the latest addition to our brain, and is a necessary and incredible gift that is responsible for critical thinking, logic, reasoning, and learning. It allows us to remember details, organize our day, and plan for tomorrow. Yet there are at least three ways that overuse of our rational mind hijacks our ability to access our deeper intuitive intelligence.

The first roadblock is the speed and volume of our thoughts. Incessant mental chatter goes from dusk until dawn and pushes out our inner signals and cues, which makes it difficult to separate intuition from thought. The rapid pace of our thought stream prevents us from seeing all angles of a problem. We enter deeper brain states when we access our nonconscious mind, as well as increase the processing speed of information, which we'll explore more extensively in Chapter 6.

To learn to reconnect with our intuition, we often have to deprogram from our default patterns of thinking, which limit our decision-making potential. In other words, we already know what we already know. In order to access new and creative solutions, we need to unlearn our thought patterns. Intuitional language operates at a different frequency, tone, and texture than thinking. It's an octave deeper. Intuition is discovered through slowing down, creating space, and listening to that still, quiet voice or sensation. It's found through paying attention to the space (intuition) between the musical notes (thinking). Our mind is programmed to focus solely on the notes themselves and not the space in between.

Through interrupting our normal way of thinking, whether by physical activity, relaxing in the sauna, going outside, or deliberate practices such as mindfulness exercises, we can begin to get some breathing room from our often random and chaotic thought stream. Then we can learn to connect with a deeper channel of information instead of reacting to every circumstance like we tend to do. This is the birthplace of outside-of-the-box thinking.

The second roadblock is that the rational mind is a limited tool and cannot grasp the fullness of life experience. The mind lives in the past (analysis and memory) or the future (imagination and projection), not the present. Yet experience happens in the present moment. Your intuitive channel is a human antenna picking up on data all around you right now. It is connected to your nonconscious mind—made up of your subconscious and unconscious—informed by feelings and sensations, and helps give you real-time intel about a person, environment, or situation. This is how Navy SEALs, professional poker players, and top salespeople excel at their professions; they know how to trust their gut when reading their surroundings.

Imagine walking into a tech firm to pitch your program that helps managers increase staff engagement and productivity through bringing in the latest social psychology and interpersonal neurobiology trends. You've spent countless hours preparing for this presentation and you don't want to blow it. This is the opportunity of a lifetime to launch your new program with such a large company.

You arrive with stacks of papers, research, and your Power-Point ready to go. As soon as you walk into the room and gauge the audience, you have a strong intuition that you need to change course on the fly. All of a sudden, you become conscious of your oversized blazer draped over your shoulders, reminding you of how your father used to rock it.

This is a young, iconoclastic, rebellious bunch that's not in the mood for another lecture. When you drop into your vibe detector and feel out the room, you realize that you need to connect in a more authentic way that speaks to the heart of their concerns and challenges around team engagement. It's time to ditch the Power-Point. This needs to be a two-way TED Talk. Are you able to trust your social intuition and read of other people on the fly? Are you able to put down the prepared speech and pivot to make room for what needs to be shared next?

This is the essence of adaptive leadership and what differentiates brilliance from the status quo. This lesson can be applied to investment pitching, sales, presentations, or team meetings. Being willing to let go of the mind's agenda and read the room is a critical intuitional skill in business and beyond. It involves trusting a deeper listening.

Relying on the mind as your only source to navigate life is like trying to use a fish net to catch water. It's the difference between observing life versus participating with it directly. Yet, this is something that I and so many others can forget throughout the course of the day. So much more information is available to us through direct experience when we are open to the vastness and richness of the present moment.

Whereas the rational mind is an incredible gift that helps us analyze and think critically, like when we are reviewing a quarterly report or designing a new system, "logic is not the only tool in your tool kit," says Doug Greene, founder of The New Hope Network and several entrepreneurial ventures. He continues, "Life is not linear nor predictable. Life is so complicated, you have to use all the tools in your toolkit. Of course you gather the logical facts you have. But the logical facts don't always have the answers. Logical facts are just another data point."[2] Doug attributes his years of success in business to developing a relationship with his intuition and integrating this resource into his daily decision-making.

Lastly, when we overidentify with our rational mind and lose touch with our inner sensations and feelings, we're locked out of our natural, intuitive state. Whether our thoughts are self-aggrandizing or self-destructive, the problem is we overidentify with them and think that this is who we are. We become biased in how we receive information and assume that what we think is true. As René Descartes said, "I think therefore I am." But this couldn't be further from the truth, as who we are is so much more than our thinking. In fact, some of the most freeing moments happen when we realize that we are not our thoughts and can get separation from the chatter, which we'll go deeper into in Chapter 5.

In addition to the rational mind as a source of important but limited information, it is also susceptible to being impacted by strong emotions and mood swings. It's not dependable when we are emotionally triggered by an event at work or going through a tough time. Our perception is less reliable in these reactive states and it's easy to become attached to our particular view. This is most evident when we perceive that we've been wronged in some way.

In order to develop a relationship with our intuition, we have to learn how to identify and separate from our thoughts. We must listen to the slower, quieter, and deeper voice within, and decode what it is saying to us.

Obstacle 2: Doubt

Another crippling obstacle that scrambles intuition is doubt. Doubt is a function of the mind and is so powerful and prevalent that it deserves its own spotlight. Doubt means second-guessing our deeper knowing. The destructive result is that we stop trusting ourselves. Doubt can creep in, especially when a situation seems risky and unfamiliar. As intuition is neither linear nor predictable, it is a threat to the control aspect of the mind, which seeks order. Doubt tries to keep us in our comfort zone.

Not trusting our inner knowing can have huge consequences. A high-end startup media company in New York City knew that it was time to expand beyond the two founders, move out of the basement office, and hire production staff and salespeople. Yet, their doubts held them back. The company lost a lot of business because they didn't believe they had what it took to manage and lead a larger team. They didn't think they could hire staff that could produce work as good as they did, which is a common fear among entrepreneurs. They eventually faced their doubts in our coaching by being willing to feel their fear and still move forward and take action, and listened to a deeper truth that led them toward grow-ing the business beyond themselves. Over time, they expanded their operations and found ways to train staff and build systems that proved their doubting minds wrong.

Doubting ourselves is incredibly disempowering and one of the main reasons why we don't act on what we feel. We become more removed from our inner intelligence and more prone to influence from or manipulation by others. The most extreme example of how we doubt ourselves is our inner critic. This aspect is such an impediment to developing a relationship with our intuition and self-authority that I've dedicated Chapter 5 to this very topic.

Doubt in the form of fear and distrust in ourselves shows up on a fundamental level with the commonly asked questions: What if my intuition is wrong? What if I have "bad" intuition? I would say that there's no such thing as bad intuition. Instead, you might have a bad *relationship* with your intuition. This distinction is important because the seduction of the mind, in order to stay in control of your system, is to convince you that you can't trust your inner compass. It will judge your intuitive nature as a threat to its supremacy and power. In fact, this is one of the main reasons people become disempowered: They doubt their intuition and inner guidance and ignore, override, or outsource their knowing to the logical mind or to the viewpoints of others.

As if the inner battle weren't enough, systems and organizations establish comfort zones as well. An employee following her intuition often puts her in conflict with those close to her. An individual's intuition in business is often met with pushback because it challenges the status quo, especially if it goes against the plan or strategy. The power to belong is such a strong force that many people doubt what they have to contribute is valuable when it challenges the company's perspective or direction.

When I interview people who identify as logical-minded—engineers, scientists, and programmers, for example—they often vehemently distrust intuition as a source of valid data and guidance. Often because it's immeasurable. And when I ask, "Do you trust your own intuition?" they usually say no. In other words, it's much safer to find objective measurements of reality to explain reality. It's an incredible risk to build a relationship with yourself and learn how to tune into and trust your inner signals. The stakes are high. You can't blame or play victim to outside data or influences for your choices. We've been conditioned out of this most critical relationship of trusting ourselves on this fundamental level. Healthy skepticism is a necessary skill because we have to cultivate our ability to think critically. Yet doubt can become a deeply embedded poison that feeds our inner critic and knocks us out of alignment with our inner navigational system, if we let it.

Daniel's story at the beginning of this chapter clearly illustrates the distrust of his intuition. He knew he needed to take on the role of CEO, yet his doubts festered because he wasn't sure he was up to the task or how this change would be received by staff. He had to wrestle with his own insecurities and fears until the pain of not taking action outweighed the pain of potentially failing.

Doubt can sometimes be mistaken for intuition. I've found that there is, however, a difference between the two. An intuitive hit is a clear message that doesn't come with a lot of emotional charge or drama. It's a feeling of obviousness, of clarity. You don't need to defend your position, make a case for it, rationalize it, or prove anything. It's simply a knowing. Doubt, on the other hand, often comes with anxiety and fear, and tends to backpedal on intuition. That's where the second-guessing, internal lawyering, and never-ending debate scrambles your conviction. With practice, you can begin to separate the clear message of an intuitive hit from the endless debates over whether you should trust what you feel.

Physical activities that demand being present, such as running, swimming, yoga, or martial arts, are incredibly helpful tools to separate intuition from doubt. Focusing on an activity does not allow space for the swirling chorus of doubts and second-guessing. I find that after a physical activity, my body is more tired and rested and my mental activity is more relaxed. Doubt subsides, and I can more easily tap into my intuitive center from this place.

Meditation and various mindfulness practices are also powerful tools to help you dis-identify with your doubts and thoughts, and you stop feeding them with your attention. Through practice, they will lose their hold over you and there is more space created for your intuition. Find the practice that speaks to you and that helps you quiet your mind. You will experience huge benefits from it.

Obstacle 3: Busyness

Busyness is a common obstacle that prevents us from sinking into our intuitive nature. Busyness is constant movement, overstimulation, the need to be entertained, overfilled schedules, and the fear of missing out that often comes from a mix of anxiety, insecurity, and a lack of self-worth. Chronic busyness is usually fueled by "doing," which leaves little room for "being."

We chase things that we don't have, such as revenue goals, fame, recognition, more leads, validation, love, Facebook likes, more market share, or higher profit margins. Underneath it all there is a deficit that we are trying to fill, or a feeling of lack. If we are not aware of what is driving our pursuits, we lose the thread of our purpose and what's meaningful to us, and it becomes an empty chase.

Busyness is also fueled by avoiding something we don't want to feel, such as anxiety about a difficult conversation with a staff member, fear of reviewing the financials, or awkwardness around making cold calls. "Shiny object syndrome" is a common term used for business leaders and managers who are easily prone to distraction as they focus on fun, easy, or new activities but don't complete any of them. They are typically avoiding something mundane or uncomfortable underneath. Whatever the scenario, staying busy is a coping strategy so you don't have to slow down and feel something difficult or uncomfortable.

I call this "go mode," and I know it all too well. When I'm in "go mode," I'm moving a million miles a minute, going from one task to the next, cramming too much into my day, and leaving no space to feel something uncomfortable that's actually driving my behavior. When I am a moving target, not only can the source of my current pain or unrest not find me, but neither can my intuition.

If I get rewarded for busyness at work, it becomes an addictive way to avoid what's happening in other parts of my life. For example, if I'm going through relationship stress or not wanting to feel my loneliness, diving fully into work mode is a coping strategy to not have to feel what's underneath my behavior.

In fact, research shows that when people are seen as busy, they are perceived as more successful and having a higher status than those who appear to have more leisure time.[3] This is the exact opposite from a century ago when more leisure time was an indicator of wealth and success. Working long and hard hours is seen as the greatest track to upward mobility and is reinforced in the media and work environments. This is how workaholics are born. In a culture where being busy is valued, we are encouraged to keep our head down and move on to the next task.

The tricky part is, pressures from work are real and deadlines and expectations can seem overwhelming. It is reasonable to think that if you slow down you will fall behind, be seen unfavorably by your team or superiors, and even risk losing your job. The key is to be accountable for your tasks, pressures, and deadlines while not getting lost in the mind's stressful narrative telling you that you cannot stop or bad things will happen.

Working longer days or spending more time staring at the computer screen is not what's needed to move through stuck places. There are moments when I can catch myself in go mode and realize that the day was a blur and I didn't feel anything as I charged through my to-dos. At that point, I start to breathe and soften, and ask myself what feelings I avoided during that time. Usually, this is the doorway into a deeper connection with myself and a wider lens from which to approach stuck places.

Busyness orients us toward outside tasks that take us away from listening to our inner guidance, which requires stillness and space to access. We are robbed of this deeper resource for decision-making as our attention is all over the place. The speed and pace of needing to get things done takes us out of the slower rhythm that's required to connect with our intuition.

Stillness is the antidote to busyness. Being still is the ability to eliminate all distractions and outside noise as well as the background mental chatter, and simply get present to your inner experience. Through this slowing down process, you become more aware of the data that your body is sending you. In a world that is moving at warp speed and filled with more information than you can take in, stillness helps you come back to your own inner essence. Learning how to be still before you take action is a very powerful tool that we'll discuss in Chapter 4. But most importantly, when you become still, you don't have to react so quickly or overfill your schedule. You are more receptive and open to what's happening in the moment, which is key to cultivating your intuition.

Overwhelm is a common result of busyness and is usually brought on by information overload or too much activity that we can't process at once. When we are in a state of overwhelm, slowing down and tuning into our intuition is almost impossible. It is one of the most common themes that my clients and I work on. Roger Bon of the University of California, San Diego, conducted a study and found that our conscious mind can hold the equivalent of thirty-four gigabytes of information per day, which is enough to overload a laptop within a matter of days.[4] Once we reach the upper limits of our capacity, we go into overwhelm, forget information, or store it in our subconscious with the risk of forgetting.

Overwhelm typically happens in business when you are multitasking. For example, checking your email, updating your project plan, and mentally preparing for your upcoming presentation while in a team meeting leaves zero room for deep listening and focusing on any of those tasks. You are not able to be fully present and therefore not able to access your deeper intuition for decision-making. David Meyer, professor of psychology at the University of Michigan, found that you can lose up to 40 percent of productivity from switching tasks.[5] This creates a snowball effect of even more overwhelm.

One of the keys to ending the vicious overwhelm cycle is to batch your time together so that you are focusing on one task at a time. Another key is to build in buffer time in your schedule. If you only schedule 75 percent of your day, you have built-in pockets of time during which you can shift gears and take a break, get outside the office, and delve into strategic thinking. Making time to work *on* your business and not just in it is the key differentiator in innovating your company or department. This allows room for a greater receptivity and openness, which is where your intuition will find you.

Obstacle 4: Fear

The fourth obstacle that prevents us from listening to our intuition is one of the most powerful emotions that drives many of our behaviors: fear. As H. P. Lovecraft famously stated, "The oldest and strongest emotion of mankind is fear, and the oldest and strongest kind of fear is fear of the unknown." He was referring to our great existential fear of death and the beyond, but fear of the unknown shows up daily. Fear is so primal that we often do what we can to avoid feeling it (staying busy is America's number-one choice). Ideally, fear is our system's warning signal that we are not safe physically, emotionally, or mentally, and it demands our attention. Fear can also show up neurotically when we are not in danger if we project our insecurities and paranoias onto our environment. This can range from subtle levels of discomfort to feeling consumed by sheer panic and terror.

Fear gets in the way of intuition because this physiological response often makes us tense, shutdown, protective, or dissociative on some level. Fear comes with a strong emotional charge throughout the body, such as tension accompanied by a compelling narrative that dominates your thoughts. Any strong emotion like anxiety, depression, rage, or shame can seize our full attention and not leave space for the quiet stillness and receptivity that is required for listening to one's intuition.

Intuition is very direct and clear, and doesn't involve extra drama or emotional intensity. Intuition requires the opposite posture to thrive, as we need a basic level of relaxation, openness, and receptivity to access this resource. Even if you receive a very strong intuitive "no" about a person or situation that feels intense, you will find that there's not a lot of story around it. It's simply a strong feeling. If you are in a situation where you are not sure if it's fear or intuition talking to you, check in and see. If there is a lot of drama and story attached to the "no," you might need to go deeper into that and feel the fear, and then see what your intuition tells you afterward.

Intuition can bring up fear as it is not coming from our conscious mind, and thus our known universe. It is outside our rational, logical thought and something we are not in control of. It is often unpredictable and may bring up powerful feelings, awarenesses, or truths that are difficult to confront. Imagine you have a strong intuition that you shouldn't take money from investors because something doesn't feel right, but you are afraid this may be your only opportunity. Or you have a gut feeling that you shouldn't go into business with a friend, yet you don't want to upset them. Would you have the courage to listen to, trust, and act on your intuition? These examples challenge core social pressures and common business practices that make it a perfect situation for fear to hijack your decision-making.

One of the most common defenses against feeling fear of the unknown is to create a comfort zone based on what is familiar. Our comfort zone is the range in which we feel safe and at ease. As creatures of habit, we form comfort zones quickly and often unconsciously in relationships, at home, at work, in how we interact with the world, in our level of risk-taking, and around what we are willing to feel and tolerate. It's a coping strategy that brings a sense of order to the chaos and unpredictability of life. Change can bring incredible amounts of anxiety and stress and is something that we sometimes resist. When we are outside of our comfort zones, we are vulnerable. We can get hurt, look like a fool, not know how to do something, or make mistakes for all to see.

The price tag is our aliveness. As Neale Walsch says, "Life begins at the end of your comfort zone."[6] Paradoxically, this is where intuition lives. It is not found in our daily thinking mindset. In other words, if we are always comfortable, we don't grow. We don't take risks to learn about ourselves and open up to new possibilities. We simply stay with what is familiar. Even if "familiar" is a dead-end job, leadership we don't respect, or a company culture that has become toxic. If we are afraid of embracing new technologies, such as digitizing our filing systems or engaging with social media, our fears will prevent us from evolving in our industry. This is why so many people stay in a job or relationship that is no longer a match, and when we do this, we die inside.

Businesses establish comfort zones all the time. In fact, being at the top can be dangerous if a company becomes complacent. There's a reason that it's hard to repeat a championship in sports or remain an industry leader. It's challenging to keep reinventing your systems, processes, and culture. It can seem like unnecessary work to revisit your vision, website, suite of services, and software solutions. Yet innovation comes from disrupting comfort zones, questioning the status quo, and catapulting beyond them. The biggest breakthroughs happen for the pioneers who are willing to venture in this unknown territory.

In Clayton Christiensen's *The Innovator's Dilemma: When New Technologies Cause Great Firms to Fail,* he observes that new organizations innovate easier with disruptive technologies because they are not tied to outdated values or organizational norms.[7] In a startup phase, there is often more room for a leader to trust his gut as he is not bogged down by bureaucracy and can make intuitive decisions on the fly. He is able to be more adaptive and stand out. Large companies end up buying smaller companies for this very reason.

Fear doesn't have to hold one back in bringing intuitive decision-making to larger organizations, however. Sherilee Joe has been in the tech industry for more than thirty years and knows how forming entrenched comfort zones gets in the way of innovative approaches to problems. She has worked as a programmer and lead cloud services architect for trailblazing companies such as Sun Microsystems, Palm, PayPal, eBay, and HP to name a few. When her team is stuck on a problem and looking for the latest bug to fix, she always encourages them to step outside of what is familiar. She is usually met with fear and resistance as she invites staff to interrupt their normal way of thinking in order to catalyze new breakthroughs. In the tech world, comfort zones usually don't include encouragement by your manager to tap into your intuition for solutions. Yet Sherilee says, "I've always known that you can only go so far intellectually. There's always another form of guidance that, if you tap into it, is very powerful."[8] She attributes this to her success of helping companies become early adopters of new technologies and guiding teams to find the source of coding problems at rapid speed.

Sherilee had no relationship to her intuition growing up. She spent years disconnected from her emotions and inner landscape. When I asked her when she became aware of her intuition, she said, "When my child was born. Whatever happened, that just opened a floodgate of emotion and feeling. It was so strong. And I was so unused to it that I thought I was heading for a nervous breakdown. I was afraid. It was so foreign to me. It was so outside my comfort zone. It was the feeling of love."[9]

Sherilee's willingness to leave her comfort zone and experience new territories gave her the confidence to teach others to face their fears and try new approaches to tackling problems. This had a huge payoff in her career and her ability to lead other staff and make an impact in technology. The ironic thing is that data and logic are usually seen as the backbone of the tech industry, but Sherilee says, "It's usually when you can see what something is and what it can leap to—that's when you have real power. Information is power. It's the power of innovation. It's the power of seeing where things are going."[10] She now helps elicit the intuition of others on her teams to create better solutions.

The more you practice leaning into your fears at work by starting with the smaller ones, you learn to overcome the obstacles in your way. This builds momentum to try new approaches and venture into new territories that were previously unfamiliar. Listening to, trusting, and acting on your intuition no matter how much fear arises will build experience and confidence, and become one of your most valuable resources over time.

Obstacle 5: Ego

The fifth obstacle that takes you out of your intuition is ego. The term *ego* is used in many different contexts and is defined here as your self-image or self-concept. In other words, it's the story you tell yourself about yourself. We all have an internalized concept of who we are based on a lifetime of conditioning from family, culture, religion, and society, and this forms your core identity of self. Ego in itself is not a bad thing. In fact, it is the organizing principle that helps you function in the world and understand your place in it. Yet your concept about who you are is different than the actual experience of who you are, or how other people experience you.

The problem occurs when you collapse the two and think you are your self-image. What often happens in business or in life is that you are trying to control the narrative of how you are perceived. This is where the ego works overtime to make sure your self-image is consistent with how you want to be seen. This can be challenging when you get locked into the idea of what it means to be a leader, manager, or a salesperson. When you are in a position of authority or demonstrating success, then you need to protect and defend this at all costs because any threat to your image can be perceived as self-annihilation. One could argue this is the cause of conflicts and wars. Being stuck in a persona of who you think you are or should be is limiting and can feel like a prison. This dynamic harms relationships because you can't bring a level of authenticity that's required for deeper relating.

So how does your ego get in the way of your intuitive nature? If you are locked into a concept of who you are and how you should behave, or when you are out just to look good, then you are not free to listen to and act on what you intuitively feel. You will block out what you sense and feel because this might not align with your social conditioning and programming. Your intuition is not bound by roles, conditions, "shoulds," obligations, or social norms.

Intuition occurs in the present moment. You get a sudden feeling in the here and now, even if it's a premonition about the future. The degree to which you are still reacting from the past about what you find acceptable or of value will directly impact your ability to listen to present-day intuition. In your family or school setting, did you have support that helped you listen to, discover, and develop a relationship with your intuition? Was your intuitive nature acknowledged? Most people don't know it's even on the menu, or they've been conditioned to ignore or push it away. We are encouraged and rewarded for an ego that is predictable and dependable. One that fits in with others. Although these are important skills, we must also continue to listen to an inner guidance that's not based on looking good or pleasing other people.

Your intuition is rooted from a deeper source of authenticity that does not care about your preferences. Intuition is not about being more comfortable or avoiding the unpleasant. It is about having the courage to say or express what you are feeling from deep within. Intuition threatens our nice little story we have about ourselves. This is great news, because we are so much more than we believe we are.

The employee that supports his boss in the meeting because he wants to get ahead but really thinks the boss is wrong, or the staff member who competes with his team to the point of creating bad blood are both examples of an ego that's running the show. Listening to and trusting your inner guidance means that you have to listen to that quieter voice that is underneath all of your insecurities, biases, assumptions, prejudices, and judgements. And that is no easy task.

The good news is that there are more tools than ever through the help of psychology and personal growth work designed to update your conditioning and help you become aware of your own biases, assumptions, and prejudices. This will help you discover how to approach the world in a way that is more in alignment with your own values and character, which is where your intuition is sourced from.

A common place for your ego to show up in business is through any type of negotiations. Whether you are negotiating a contract, a business deal, an equity distribution, or a partnership, listening to your intuition serves a radically different outcome than one that is only centered around your personal ego. Ego used in a healthy way is a powerful and necessary force that provides the drive and energy that helps you stay on target toward your goals, which ideally are aligned with your values and inner compass. Ego used in unhealthy ways employs your willpower to dig in your heels, not wanting to be wrong, being inflexible, not considering others, and prioritizing your agenda over the ecosystem that you are negotiating inside of.

One of the core principles of listening to your intuition involves a willingness to surrender your will and personal agenda to a deeper guidance within. This can seem antithetical to business principles if you are only focused on personal gains or the bottom line. Yet, we are entering an era in which a business that is used solely as a vehicle for shareholders' value and profit is not sustainable. Now more than ever, companies that want to retain employees are tasked with creating a meaningful vision, company culture, and benefits that demonstrate staff are cared for and valued. This win-win approach gets genuine engagement and buy-in from your team.

Intuition operates at a different frequency than the ego. No matter how driven we are to achieve something, we can't impose our will if we want to be in a relationship with what is happening around us. Intuition is about slowing down, listening, and tuning in to a different rhythm than our typical egocentric mentality. Successful entrepreneurs and negotiators find that being able to listen to what wants to happen in a negotiation is the key principle to a win-win outcome.

Stephan Rechtschaffen, cofounder of the Omega Institute and founder of the retreat center Blue Spirit Costa Rica, is familiar with the power of listening to something deeper than his personal ego in a business context from his years of negotiations and deals. Cultivating a relationship with his intuition has allowed him to listen to what feels right in a given situation and honor the flow of all the stakeholders and the greater ecosystem.

> *If I'm trying to serve only whatever my needs might be in this moment, I'm moving further away from what we could call a win-win outcome. If I'm dealing with someone else in a business negotiation, we've now entered into something where there's a "we." It's like being in a relationship with your spouse or partner. I have a certain perspective; my wife has a certain perspective; and the relationship holds a certain perspective. So how do we do that? In business, it's really important to see beyond oneself if one is not doing that. Then we are developing our inner listening, which gives us an opportunity to think outside the box.[11]*

Stephan demonstrates how we can apply deeper listening skills to enhance our intuition in business negotiations. He knows that when both sides of the table feel honored, respected, and listened to, and are participating in the conversation, they are likely to form stronger partnerships based on trust. Going beyond his personal ego to get the most out of a situation has earned him greater wins in the long term for himself, his colleagues, and in partnerships. The issue of sustainability is one of the most critical topics of our time and immediately puts all of us in a "we" perspective. Listening to our intuitive voice allows for more authentic communication and trust between investors, board members, conflicts, partner disputes, pitching, and a greater resonance with our ecosystem.

In business as in life, there is a place for the ego and how it helps us organize our reality. The problems arise when we confuse the story we tell about ourselves as absolute truth. Then we need to defend, jostle, get ahead, look good, avoid taking responsibility, and a myriad of other behaviors that are only aimed at our self-preservation. In listening to and acting from our intuitive center, we are able to approach business from a larger perspective that doesn't just include our own needs, but all stakeholders involved.

Conclusion

The rational mind, doubt, busyness, fear, and the ego disconnect you from your intuitive nature and inner compass. They crowd out the space in their own distinct ways and make it incredibly challenging to make choices from the natural state of your intuitive knowing. By recognizing when one of these obstacles gets in the way of being more present to what your inner signals are trying to communicate, you have an opportunity to pivot and drop deeper into your inner guidance, and make better decisions as a result. Now that you've explored the chief obstacles, let's look at the steps to connecting and building a relationship with your intuition.

You Don't Find Your Intuition; Your Intuition Finds You

3

The intellect has little to do on the road to discovery. There comes a leap in consciousness, call it intuition or what you will, and the solution comes to you and you don't know why or how.

—Albert Einstein

Lisa was twenty-nine weeks pregnant with Avery when she and her husband headed down the mountain from Summit County, Colorado, into Denver. It was their last big date night before they would be a family of three. As they made their way down the winding mountain road, the car jerked and they heard the deafening sound of an impact. It was a hit and run. When they pulled over, they were in shock but relieved that they both seemed okay. But soon Lisa started to feel contractions. She was in labor.

The planned dinner turned into an emergency visit to the hospital. They called for an ambulance, and when the ambulance arrived at the hospital, the paramedics wheeled her in immediately. Doctors prescribed a high dose of muscle relaxers to try and stop the contractions. However, they could only give Lisa so much because of how far along she was in the pregnancy. Lisa was told that she couldn't move because there was a chance the placenta had dislodged. There she was, in shock, strapped to a hospital bed, terrified about the fate of her unborn child. Despite being a trained trauma therapist, she was frozen with fear and entirely reliant on the expertise of the doctors and nurses around her.

Having a baby at twenty-nine weeks is a dangerous proposition. Lisa was doing her best to calm down, but she was still in a state of panic. Next to the hospital bed were two monitors. One was tracking her vitals, and the other was tracking Lisa's unborn daughter, Avery. Lisa was mesmerized by those monitors. She fixated on whether they were aligned or out of sync and whether either of them was spiking. The monitors reflected both the state of their relationship with each other, as well as the disconnection Lisa was experiencing inside herself.

An unsettling pattern was in progress: Whenever the doctors gave muscle relaxers to Lisa, her body calmed down and the contractions dissipated. Then, each time the medicine wore off, the contractions started again. And the cycle continued.

Lisa gave her authority over to the doctors and nurses. She feared that Avery would be born premature and then confined to an incubator, where Lisa couldn't hold her. Like many of us under severe stress, Lisa lost connection with herself. She was frozen. Her husband also was an anxious mess, unable to support her.

Then something changed. Lisa became pissed. Being strapped to a bed wasn't right! That feeling was the beginning of her inner guidance system kicking in again. She was livid, and her body wanted to move.

After two days in the hospital managing her contractions and trying to stop the birth process, the nurse finished her 2:00 a.m. shift and left Lisa. Alone, Lisa declared to herself, "I'm done. I'm done with this shit." She unstrapped herself, keeping only the sensors that were needed to measure her vitals, and broke free from the bed that felt like a prison. She followed her intuition. She moved, stretched, and let her body unwind and connect back with herself. She later shared with me, "Telling someone not to move after a trauma when their body instinctively and wisely needs to move is the worst thing you can do because the energy stays stuck in the system. The body needs to unwind through the trauma."

As she allowed her body to do what it needed to do, she happened to walk by a floor-length mirror. She took in her appearance: hospital gown, distended belly, and in labor. The reality that she had only one more dose of the muscle relaxers left loomed over her. That was it. She needed to get control of her contractions right away or she would be delivering Avery. *It's up to me*, she said to herself.

In that moment, the full reality of the situation hit Lisa like a loud boom, and her intuition kicked in with full force. Lisa took a deep breath and went inside herself to connect and energetically find her baby. "I found Avery in that moment," she later told me. "Not her physical body but something deeper. We reconnected."

Dance, a loud voice from inside Lisa commanded her. So, at 2:00 a.m., in a hospital gown and scared, she started to dance with her daughter inside her. They connected. And she felt her nervous system unwind. She felt the two of them sync up.

She stopped listening to everybody else, and her intuition found her. After the dance, she got back in the bed and fell asleep.

The next morning, Lisa's contractions picked up again, and she received the final dose of muscle relaxers. Either the contractions would stop or she would deliver the baby. Someone came in with a waiver for her to sign for the operating room. Everyone was mobilizing while Lisa lay there terrified. Once again, she was confronted with the question of where she was going. Was she going to listen to herself or listen to everyone else around her? When she looked over at the monitors one last time, the vital signs were going bonkers. She remembers hearing a stirring inside herself shout, *No! No! Today's not the day Avery is going to be born!*

Lisa closed her eyes and blocked everybody and everything out. While chaos swirled around her, she focused on the rhythm of the dancing. When she focused on her intuition and the rhythm of her body and the connection with Avery, the contractions stopped. She gained control of her internal chaos, and calmed her baby and her body through her connection with her intuition. She and Avery, still inside her, went home that afternoon. Avery was born at thirty-nine weeks, happy and healthy.

Connecting to her intuition in the middle of her crises completely changed the trajectory of Lisa's life. She created synergetic play therapy (SPT), a therapy model centered on training therapists to listen and follow their intuition when working with children. She stated, "You can't do SPT unless you are relying on your intuition that guides you step by step. It's the intuitive piece, the therapist's ability to work with herself, that allows the therapist to know what to do to support the healing in another being."[1] Avery wasn't supposed to be born that night, but that was the night that SPT was born.

Lisa's incredible story highlights how critical listening to intuition is and how difficult doing that can be when chaos and fear are dominating and other people are telling us what to do. Yet, as Lisa demonstrated, eliminating outer and internal distractions is possible. We just need to go inside and connect with ourselves at the deepest level. This is critical when doing business.

In today's business environment of high expectation and instant results, there are many outside pressures. Often, the focus is on survival. Leaders and managers find themselves overriding their inner compasses while they fight "fires." The US Bureau of Statistics reports that only 50 percent of small businesses survive the first five years and 30 percent survive the first ten years of existence.[2] And a 2012 study by Harvard Business School lecturer Shikhar Ghosh estimated that three out of every four venture-backed firms fail.[3]

Even in the most critical moments, the way leaders respond can make all the difference. If someone reacts from panic or fear, he or she has limited options and possibilities. To paraphrase Abraham Maslow, when you're a hammer, everything looks like a nail.[4] Yet when we stay connected to and aware of our inner signals and needs, we can pivot quickly and reach new potential.

Connecting deeply with oneself in stressful situations is required to go beyond reactivity and toward resilience and strength. Intuition can serve as the grounded wisdom that is so desperately needed in chaotic environments. Making that connection is one of the most profound, self-empowering experiences available to you in a business setting. It opens up opportunities to bring more of yourself to your work and to add tremendous value to the culture and direction of your company. Yet, outsourcing your business instincts and decision-making to those who have more seniority, those who are higher up on the organizational chart, or investors, shareholders, or board members can be so easy.

Your inner navigational system provides direction, discernment, and the ability to help you to make clear, lightning-quick decisions. In business, that ability coupled with critical thinking is an incredible advantage. Your team will be able to pivot, on a moment's notice, based on a careful read of the competitive landscape, the needs of the target market, and effective communication with staff.

But the creation of such a highly adaptive culture starts with encouraging the development of each staff member's inner landscape and intuitive skill set. Letting go of implicit biases and standard ways of seeing markets and customers, in order to view new opportunities from a fresh perspective, requires effort. To make room for that effort the leadership team needs to lead by example. Let's dive into the first of the six steps in cultivating a relationship with your intuitive center: shifting your perspective to receptivity.

Step 1: You Don't Find Your Intuition; Your Intuition Finds You

What is the first step in connecting with your intuition? Shifting your orientation from doing to being. From goal-oriented action to openness and receptivity. This step is about reducing your attention to the outside world and instead tuning in to the conversation within yourself.

Intuition isn't something you achieve or accumulate. It also isn't a goal you attain. Seeking an answer from your inner guidance system by trying to force a connection won't work. But that's the typical American and Western approach: Go after what we want and don't stop until we achieve our dreams. Living that way is ingrained in American society. Yet, there are some situations when activity gets in the way of receptivity. In other words, you don't find your intuition; your intuition finds you.

When you create enough space to be receptive, you allow your deeper intelligence to find you. If you're always a moving target, how can your inner guidance system find you? In other words, if your attention is constantly occupied, grinding through your to-do list, and bombarded by media and entertainment, how can you listen to your needs and the creativity that may want to express itself through you? How can there be room for innovative possibilities and open-ended strategic thinking if you're constantly filling your life with digital devices and movement?

The average smartphone user checks his or her phone about 221 times per day.[5] This growing dependency makes tuning in to intuition challenging. Listening to your inner landscape and what your internal social media is posting in real time is difficult. We need to slow down and not let adrenaline, caffeine, and anxiety dominate daily life. It's no wonder that we get some of our best ideas when we're in the shower, walking in nature, meditating, or reflecting. When we slow down and cultivate receptivity, something relaxes inside of us, allowing a deep wisdom to come through.

This first step in connecting with your intuition is critical. It's about reorienting yourself from the go-go-go mentality. If you need to get new prospects to fill your pipeline and you're not sure which marketing agency to invest in, you might feel overwhelmed, make an impulsive decision, and force something to happen. If you hire a new employee quickly, you run a high risk of him or her being a poor hire. If you don't slow down and allow yourself to be guided by the deep knowing inside, you may make an ill-informed decision. Such a decision—especially a really big one—can be costly.

Steven Rogall, CEO of Rogall Painting, illustrates this point effectively.[6] His business was growing rapidly, and he urgently needed to hire a manager to oversee the crews. He had a friend (we'll call him Devon) whom he was considering for the position. Devon was experienced in the field, but Steven had reservations about hiring him. He knew that Devon had a track record of inconsistency; he acted one way in front of you but another way behind your back.

Steven pulled the trigger anyway, overriding his intuition. At first, Devon got along well with the members of the team, and they seemed to appreciate his leadership. But, Steven had a feeling that there was a problem. In fact, every time he saw Devon, he felt a sense of distrust. He continually brushed off the feeling, telling himself it was just in his head.

Soon enough, morale changed. The employees started to ignore Steven's direction. And although they told Steven that everything was fine whenever he asked, his inner radar told him otherwise. Eventually, one of the employees told Steven that Devon was polluting the team and complaining nonstop about the company and Steven—even to the customers. He had been actively creating discord!

Devon was a toxic element, and he had infected four employees under him. Yet, to Steven's face, he was happy and easygoing. The outward data didn't support what Steven's gut was telling him, which was that he needed to get rid of this guy. Steven soon realized Devon had a stronger relationship with his team than he did. He realized how much he wasn't connecting with his own team.

Finally, Steven admitted he could no longer trust Devon, and he got rid of him. As a result of the toxic environment that Devon had created, he also let four other employees go. Steven told me that if he had trusted his intuition, those four people might still be employed by his company. If he had given them the right leader, he might have been able to keep them.

This experience was the pivotal turning point in Steven's business. He realized that he needed to make himself accountable. He wasn't following his gut, and that was costly in terms of being understaffed and having to replace employees. It took a while for him to undo some of the effects that Devon had on the company culture. Steven vowed never to shut out his intuition again. Several years later, Rogall Painting is thriving, with a strong company culture, brand, and reputation.

Steven shared that, in hindsight, if he had slowed down and made time to listen to his intuition, he never would have hired Devon in the first place. We can all learn from Steven's experience. It takes a big shift in mindset to slow down and be receptive to what you're sensing and feeling. Intuition isn't something you need to hunt down. In my experience, intuition is waiting for you to listen. It's waiting for a quiet, receptive moment. All you need to do is create space for it. When you soften your orientation from doing to being, you open yourself to the profound wisdom inside yourself.

Intuition is like those 3-D image prints that, at first, look like a bunch of dots. When your eyes are too focused on the image and you're too close to it, you can't make out any pattern. But as soon as you take a few steps back and soften your gaze, the 3-D image emerges. You can use a similar approach to train yourself to seek your intuition. Don't pursue your intuitive guidance so intently. Instead, create a gentle, relaxing receptivity that invites your deeper guidance to knock gently on the door to your consciousness.

Let's take a moment to learn from Marc David's experience, as he takes us back to the moment in his life when he created space for his intuition to find him and, in doing so, pioneered a new field within his industry. That moment was the catalyst for his health and nutrition training and certification program, The Institute for the Psychology of Eating.

There was a point where I was asking the universe and life what was next for me. I was a freelance cowboy. I was doing a combination of one-on-one counseling with clients, corporate consulting in health and nutrition and wellness education, and advising corporate wellness programs. I was also doing marketing consulting and traveling a lot. I was getting tired of that lifestyle. I was also doing a lot of teaching and guest teaching in other people's organizations. I knew something had to shift.

I had just gotten divorced, and my son was living with his mom. Our agreement was that he comes to me in four more years, when he's thirteen years old. And I thought to myself, I can't be traveling this much when I'm a full-time dad. I felt at a loss as to what to do next. There was a growing anxiety as I felt this restlessness of really wanting some answers.

And then, one day, I was out on a walk while all of these questions were swirling around. I found a rock to sit on and just let myself get really quiet and drop all of my mental stories. And, after a while, an intuition came through really strong and said clearly, "You're going to start your own institute and take the body of work you've created and organize it in a whole different way. People will be coming to you rather than you going to them, so that you can be in one place and ground yourself."

As the answers to my questions came through, my initial response was this wave of "Wow! That feels so big and so right!" Followed by this wave of "Oh, my God. There are like 29,000 steps to make that happen." I'm smart enough to know how much work that's going to be. What came through in that intuition scared the bejeezus out of me. But I also knew it was correct. I then waited for the right moment to strike to put it all into action.

What I've created now is a multi-million-dollar business that does very well and supports seventeen people and their families. Between our social media platforms and mailing list, we reach millions of people each week. We do good work in the world. We help people. We have an Eating Psychology Coach training for professionals, and we have another program for anyone who wants to work on their relationship with food. Graduates' lives are changed. The lives of their patients and clients are changed.

And all of this was from an intuition that had me quaking in my boots. I started an organization that I had no idea how I was going to roll out. Sometimes when I get an intuition, it doesn't give me all the details of how I'm going to do it. It just gives me the target I'm supposed to hit. Like, move to Boulder, Colorado. Organization and movement start to happen as I buy in.[7]

Sitting on that rock, Marc experienced a transitional moment in his life. Fear and resistance stop many of us from listening to and acting on our inner guidance. Instead of making an impulsive decision to avoid his discomfort or just doing what others around him thought he should do, Marc changed his perspective. He opened up to a deep reservoir of intelligence inside himself. That one shift of perspective, which came from getting into nature, stopping, and reflecting, opened up a new doorway outside his everyday mindset.

The following exercises can help you find practical ways to practice shifting your perspective and allowing room and space for your intuition to find you.

Exercise 1: Walk Around the Block

When you find yourself easily distracted at work or staring at the computer screen for too long, it's time to change things up. Shifting your attention can be incredibly helpful to keep your mind fresh and open to new possibilities. A perspective shift is also critical when you have focused on a specific type of tactical work and you need to change gears to more strategic thinking. Strategic thinking requires a different mindset. This exercise will help you shift your perspective so that your intuition can find you.

Interrupt Your Routine

Remove yourself from your desk. Do whatever is necessary to let people know that you'll be unavailable for thirty minutes (or however long you need). That is great practice for setting boundaries and self-care, which can be really hard for some people. To make the most of this time, turn off the notifications and ringers on your electronic devices so that you can be present in your experience. If you respect this time and space, you'll reap the rewards.

Move Your Body

Take a walk outside your office space, if possible. If you're in a residential area, find a route that inspires you but doesn't overstimulate you. If you're in the middle of a major metropolitan area, find a park or trail nearby. Set a timer to go off when you need to make your way back, so that you don't need to actively check your phone.

Get Present

As you walk your route, let your thoughts about the day go and immerse yourself fully in the present moment. The key is to get out of your normal way of thinking and allow for more open awareness and slower movement. Feel each of your steps land on the ground. That will help to keep your attention in the moment. When you slow down physically, you tend to take in more information.

Breathe

Take several deep breaths, and relax into each step you take. The more you let go of your thoughts and return to your breathing and the feel of your feet on the ground, the more present you will be in the moment. Doing this takes practice, but as you practice, you're shifting from doing to being.

Slow Down

Walk at a slower pace than you usually do. Notice what happens when you purposely slow down and choose to be present in your experience. Let yourself feel each step, from the heel of the foot to the toes, as you slow down from your normal pace. What do you notice? What is the quality of your breathing? Where does your attention go naturally? How do other people around you seem when you slow down?

Ask Yourself a Question

Once you slow down and find a rhythm, ask yourself some questions. This is the perfect opportunity for the large decisions you're facing. Whether you're considering hiring a new employee, which CRM to go with, why customer complaints are on the rise, or why your director's behavior feels off to you, this is the moment to ask those questions and stay with them. Try to just let the question rest in your mind. We have a tendency to seek an answer, to figure out the right choice. But intuition shies away from that type of demanding approach. Instead, hold the question lightly in your mind and let your intuition find you. After a while, something unexpected may arise.

...

Do this exercise whenever you need to get into a different mindset and think strategically. As a business coach, I've worked with hundreds of high-performing but trouble-making clients, and if there is a communication breakdown, I never take meetings with them in an office. I learned the hard way that if I want to make any progress we need to get the hell out of the office, where all the problems exist. If I can, I take us into nature or quiet streets nearby. This simple change of environment can make all the difference in relaxing a person and getting him or her out of the normal perspective and moving toward new possibilities.

Steve Jobs was famous for walking around his neighborhood barefoot whenever he was pondering a big change. I worked with a CEO who did a walkabout almost daily and certainly whenever he was facing tough decisions or wanted creative inspiration. Through practice, he trained himself to enter a creative space immediately. He also encouraged his employees to take walks for the same reasons. That sort of walking became part of his company culture. Anyone could step away from what he or she was working on. He treated his employees like adults and respected their choices to think strategically while still performing their tactical duties. The employees succeeded in coming up with creative solutions that benefited the company. Walking with one another was also a great way to settle conflicts, because it enabled employees to get out of their usual mindsets and listen to one another in a different way.

During one of my on-site visits to this company, I learned that one employee had become argumentative and, at times, defiant in company meetings. He brought a lot of value to the team, but his negativity was causing problems and becoming toxic. My intuition told me that I needed to get that employee out of the office. We walked through the quiet neighborhood streets nearby. I deepened my breath to settle myself down, which I know from experience settles down other people as well.

At first, he was suspicious. He grilled me about my intentions. But then his own breath started to match mine, and he relaxed. He shared with me some of the stresses and concerns that had been building inside him. I listened and created a nonjudgmental space in which he could feel safe. In response to that, he became receptive to my feedback. He felt that I was truly trying to help him succeed. Sometime after our conversation, he took on a manager position and became a great team player and supporter of the company culture. I'm not sure how much of his attitude change was directly related to our exchange, but I'm confident that we made a real connection. And clearly something in him changed. He felt heard and understood.

I've seen this a hundred times. When there is space for problematic employees to be heard and understood, they often turn themselves around. But we have space for others inside us only when we first have space for ourselves. I'll talk more about that in a bit.

A change in your perspective can happen when you shift your environment by going outside. But you don't always have to go outside to do that. What else can you do to interrupt your routine if your thoughts are spinning in an unproductive direction? Five minutes of exercise can get your blood flowing. A simple breathing exercise of breathing in deeply, holding that breath in for five seconds, and then exhaling it for another five seconds can help you calm down. Try the breathing exercise for five minutes. You'll be surprised at how much you calm down and feel capable of tackling the challenge in front of you. You may be only one perspective shift away from finding a new, powerful solution.

Another way you can practice receptivity is by pausing before firing back a response. Many of us have been trained to respond right away when someone asks us a question in the workspace, because deadlines are looming and other pressures have built up.

We rarely take a moment to consciously slow down and say, "You know, give me a second to think about that." But doing that will allow space for intuitive solutions to find us. If you're managing an employee and that employee comes to you asking several questions in a frenetic way, try the next exercise.

Exercise 2: Take a Pause

Before responding to a question or problem, slow things down, take a pause, and see what answers come to you. The best answer may not be your first thought.

Create Space

Take a breath and create a moment of silence before you answer. Sometimes you may even need to ask the other person to slow down and repeat the question. A lot of times, employees don't realize that they're carrying so much anxiety or stress because they're in a reactive state. Don't let yourself get sucked into that dynamic. If you do, your response will match the other person's reactive mode. By setting a boundary, you will honor your own pace of processing information, and your calmer nervous system will help your employee to calm down as well. We're social animals, and our states affect the states of those around us.

Go Within

Do a quick inventory of what you're feeling in the moment. Try to separate the questioner's need to know from your own internal search for a potential solution. Take a breath. What happens when you let the question sit inside you? What does your inner intelligence tell you? You may need more time to respond, so be willing to say so if that's the case. Keep breathing and let yourself relax into the question.

Notice What Stands Out

Once you pause, create space, and avoid reactive problem-solving, consider what you're feeling. What's coming to you? What do you feel moved to share with the other person? What does your gut say?

Trust your inner radar. It will guide the conversation to where it needs to go. Following your inner radar can be especially difficult in meetings. Yet, whenever a leader takes the time to listen to a question and really ponder it, everyone else in the room feels a sense of gravity and respect because the leader is truly considering the situation. By honoring themselves with a pause, such leaders train others to do the same.

Respond

Make the call about whether you should answer the question. Do you have an answer? Do you have follow-up questions? The best approach may be to bounce the same question back to the person, to train him or her in how to think critically. For example, if someone approaches you and asks, "What should I do about our upcoming deadline? I'm afraid we're not going to make it!" you can respond by taking a breath and pausing. That alone may open up new possibilities for intuition to find you or the other person. Then you can ask, "What do you think we should do?" or "If I wasn't here, what would you suggest as a next step?"

Answering questions on their own helps people avoid becoming too dependent on your leadership and to begin cultivating their own. Pausing for a moment and creating space to think from a different perspective can open up new possibilities. This approach is also incredibly useful with confrontations. By taking a pause, you give yourself a moment to think about how you want to react, and you can shift the entire conversation. When you pause and don't allow yourself to be reactive, you can lead toward a new resolution and shared understanding. Take a moment to breathe deeply and reflect before you fire off a hasty email that you'll regret later. I know the importance of that from personal experience!

There are many times you can practice pausing in a business environment. In every situation, there is a little space to change perspective and consider new possibilities. When we interrupt the usual modes of being, we shift our ways of thinking and responding and make room for the deeper intelligence within to find us.

Receptivity makes a huge difference in business meetings and one-on-one sessions. When you're totally present, you deepen your work relationships. Other people will feel that you're really listening to them. Thought leaders such as Simon Sinek are speaking out about this. In an interview, Simon said, "If you are sitting in a meeting with people you are supposed to be listening and speaking to, and you put your phone on the table, that sends a subconscious message to the room 'you're just not that important.'"[8] Unfortunately, people do this all too often.

Effective communication and management aren't just about setting direction and making decisions. They're about connecting authentically with other people. And the more present you are for each person, the more that person will feel valued and respected in your organization. Receptivity can build trust and loyalty better than any bonus or incentive plan can.

In fact, Steven Rogall made the following adamant statement to me:

Leadership is people. It's your influence on people. It's not just numbers and data. That's the easiest part. If you go through a two-year MBA program, I guarantee you that that's the easiest part of the process. The most difficult part and the most confronting is dealing with yourself. That will take you on a whole other ride. That's the real work that needs to happen.

If I can't connect with what's real inside of me, I can't connect with what's real inside of you either. Better said, I can't help you connect with what's real inside of you. Because I'm not an example of that. I don't stand as source for that. If I lead by example, then it's a different story. I can only go as deep with other people, in connection, as I've gone with myself.

When you are leading people, that's what creates loyalty and culture and all of those things inside the business. When you look at the Gallup poll and the lack of engagement in companies, almost all of those questions have to do with the relationship with the direct report and the manager. And it isn't really just about task-oriented stuff. That's the easiest part of the job. It's the connection part that's key. People don't leave companies; they leave their managers.[9]

Conclusion

Practicing this one step of changing your perspective toward receptivity will have huge ramifications for you in business. By walking around the block and getting fresh air whenever your mind is stuck or on repeat, creating space by taking a pause rather than responding automatically, and letting your surroundings peer into you, you shift from your normal orientation, which can be narrowly focused, to a more open, vast awareness where insights await you. When you allow space for your curiosity and questions, your deep inner wisdom can find you. The first step of becoming more receptive prepares you for the next step of connecting with your inner guidance system: slowing down.

Slowing Down *Is* an Action Step

Intuition will tell the thinking mind where to look next.

—Dr. Jonas Salk

Mike Orlando[1] could feel the veins popping out of his forehead under the California sun as he walked home, fresh from an all-out fight with his boss. As his shock thawed out, his anger grew as he replayed what just happened.

Mike had been working as an analytical chemist in the UC system for ten years, most recently at UC Santa Barbara, and assumed that this was his career path. He was in charge of a research project studying pollution levels of local watersheds. They collected more than 760 samples of water composition in the area. He diligently worked long hours to record and file all of the samples properly before the Christmas break, and felt great that he made his deadline.

As soon as he walked into the lab on January 2nd, his boss tore into him. Mike couldn't even get a word in. He was shocked because he had worked incredibly hard to complete his research and his boss was chewing him out for no reason. When there was a break in the barrage, he asked what his boss was so upset about. His boss continued to blast him and accused him of sabotaging the samples and the research that he had worked so hard to complete.

As the abuse continued, Mike was bewildered, shocked, and offended at the accusation, and all he could do in that moment was flip his middle finger at his boss and storm out. He went straight to the department chair's office to report what had happened. The chair recommended they hold a meeting the next day to get to the bottom of what was going on.

Mike was fuming and his thoughts were racing. His whole career path and everything that he had been building toward was now altered forever. He knew he couldn't go back to that type of environment. For all intents and purposes, he had quit the moment he gave his boss the finger. But what would he do? His brain scrambled for possibilities.

Mike walked the four miles home as he needed to let off some steam. About halfway there, he noticed how stressed out he was. His blood pressure was rising, veins were popping, and thoughts were swirling, all fueled by equal parts of anger, stress, and anxiety. His whole life was changing and panic was setting in. He didn't know what was next and had no clue what he would do to make money. He wanted to bring his passions into creating something that he loved.

Then something out of the ordinary happened. He began to slow down. This wasn't intentional, but he followed the urge to take a moment and collect himself. He took a few breaths for what felt like the first time all day. He started to feel his body again. His feet on the pavement. The sun on his back. As he gained some perspective, he was amused on some level of how bizarre this moment seemed.

As he slowed down, he took a moment and looked at the environment around him. The cars moved on the street at a snail's pace. The leaves of the trees became more distinct. And something inside of him started to relax. Although he had done this walk hundreds of times, everything was in slow motion as the transition of his life was hitting him in a new way. Although waves of panic were naturally having their way with him a moment ago, he was able to find calmness in the storm. And that's when a bolt of passion and inspiration struck him in a profound way that would change the course of his life: chocolate.

That's right, chocolate. Immediately he heard this message and had a whole-body experience that stopped him in his tracks. It was an unmistakable feeling of rightness. That's the moment when the idea to turn his side hobby into a business became clear. That's when he decided to become a chocolate maker.

He flashed back to a time in high school when he thought, "I don't even know what chocolate is! I have no idea where it comes from. Is it a plant? Is it a bean? What is it?"[2] The scientist in him came alive as he did more research and started to pursue chocolate-making as a hobby. But he never intended for it to be his business.

In this moment, however, pursuing a chocolate-making business felt right. This was the last thing he expected given the whirlwind of the day. He felt a weight lift off of his chest. He didn't know how it would work as he had never run his own business before, but something just felt right about this in a very deep way. He knew that he had the smarts and the commitment to make it happen.

Mike showed up at the department chair's office the next day, and his supervisor was again blaming him for the mix-up in samples and sabotaging the research that they had all spent countless hours on. Mike was amazed that he was getting thrown under the bus, while everyone else in the lab knew that it was the field researchers who were careless in collecting samples and had ruined some of the control group studies. They were just young students and didn't have the same level of care that more experienced scientists brought to the field. Regardless, Mike didn't feel like defending himself. He knew that his boss and the chair were friends and that he wouldn't want to work for someone who turned on him like this. The trust was broken. He was done.

He formally quit at that meeting and again walked the four miles home. This time he felt more clear and relaxed. He had a good feeling about chocolate and felt confident it was going to work out, even though he didn't know how he would do it. All of his chips were in. He called his girlfriend at the time and told her he quit.

After telling her the story, he said matter-of-factly and out loud for the first time, "Well, it looks like I'm going to be a chocolate maker!" And just like that his entrepreneurial vision was launched. He budgeted a year to get to breakeven sales before his money would run out. And in late January of 2010, he launched Twenty-Four Blackbirds Chocolates in downtown Santa Barbara. It started as a small-batch, bean-to-bar chocolate company. (It was also serendipitous timing as he launched the company right when the "new American craft chocolate movement" was gaining traction.) What started in his kitchen with a pound of cocoa beans, a juicer, and a toaster oven has now turned into a small-scale artisan chocolate company, complete with a factory stocked with home-built or modified equipment, serving more than 400 retail customers nationwide.

Mike's background as a scientist who utilizes his intuition gave him a distinct advantage as he integrated the best of both worlds.

Using my intuition with my science background is the advantage. My background in science gives me an advantage over other chocolate makers. For example, when it comes to hand processing, our output per unit time is much higher than everybody else's. I am left- and right-brained. I live and breathe science. I see no reason not to add artistic approaches to scientific methods. It's worked for me up until now. I have a successful business, so something is working. If I was totally washed up from a series of bad decisions, I'd have to rethink this. But it's been the opposite. It's worked out.[3]

Mike attributes intuition as the driver for all of his creative thoughts and innovation. In fact, Mike invented two new pieces of equipment used to make chocolate that he sells to other companies. His intuition speaks to him in his dreams. "I'll wake up from a dream and realize I've dreamt a schematic for a machine. Then I'll immediately get myself up and draw it." And soon after, he'll bring the drawing to life and engineer the equipment himself.

As a business leader, he inherently trusts his intuition and it continues to serve him. Twenty-Four Blackbirds Chocolates is now distributed internationally, and he recently moved into a new factory that triples as a wholesale distributor, a retail store, and a chocolate cafe. He attributes his success to that one day under the

California sun when he found the time to slow down, get underneath his ruminating thoughts, and discover the insight that would spark a whole new trajectory in his life.

As Mike's story shows, once you set the stage by changing your orientation and mindset to being more open and receptive, the second step in deepening access to your intuition is to slow down. In today's world, slowing down is seen as a negative, especially in the business world. It can be seen as unproductive, something that keeps you behind your competition, something that prohibits you from staying relevant in the marketplace, or something that happens when you get older and are "off your game." Yet, most often the biggest breakthroughs reported by innovators and entrepreneurs occur when they slow down their normal way of thinking and processing information, which allows space for other sources of data to catch up to them.

Carl Honoré refers to this as "slow thinking" in his book, *In Praise of Slow*. "Slow thinking is intuitive, woolly, and creative. It is what we do when the pressure is off, and there is time to let ideas simmer on the back burner. It yields rich, nuanced insights and sometimes surprising breakthroughs."[4] You need the discipline of carving out quiet time and space to listen. To get curious. To be still. To be able to relax and settle into this deeper intelligence.

We often complain that we don't have time to slow down, yet we do nothing to change that. So what we need to do is redefine what it means to be productive. Stanford researcher John Pencavel published a study showing that productivity begins to fall off at about fifty hours per week.[5] This shows that we are trending in the wrong direction if we think longer hours equals more productivity. So instead of thinking of relaxing and slowing down as doing nothing or being unproductive, what if you saw this as an opportunity to reset your attention and optimize your efforts? Slowing down is an action step. It takes conscious attention and focus to be able to block out the external speed and noise so that you can tune into what's happening internally.

Intuition operates at a different rhythm than our daily thoughts, and at an octave deeper. And intuition, the wellspring of innovation, occurs when we are able to slow down our normal beta brain wave states and enter deeper alpha and theta states. Meditation and the flow states that athletes, musicians, artists, and performers practice can take us to altered brain states where we can access our nonconscious mind and improve performance.[6] The nonconscious mind is where we store most of our information and experiences, and where our intuition can find us. Innovative companies like Google are bringing these practices to their teams to improve performance, decision-making, and innovative thinking.

University of Amsterdam psychologist Ap Dijksterhuis and his colleagues confirmed the power of slowing down to access our nonconscious thought to make better decisions.[7] He exposed subjects to complex information about potential apartments, roommates, or art posters.

The researchers invited some participants to state their immediate preference after reading, say, a dozen pieces of information about each of four apartments. A second group, given several minutes to analyze the information consciously, tended to make slightly smarter decisions. But wisest of all, in study after study, was a third group, whose attention was distracted for a time—enabling the subjects' minds to process the

complex information unconsciously and to achieve more or-
ganized and crystallized judgments, with more satisfying re-
sults. Faced with complex decisions involving many factors,
the best advice may indeed be to take our time—to "sleep
on it"—and to await the intuitive result of our unconscious
processing.[8]

The paradox is: When you allow time to slow down for your intuition to find you, you arrive at a decision more quickly. By relaxing your mind and accessing your deeper consciousness, the answer is already there, waiting for you. How could it be possible that by slowing down you can arrive at a decision faster and more accurately? Neuroscience shows us that the subconscious mind processes twenty million environmental stimuli per second versus forty interpreted by the conscious mind.[9] That's not a typo. Our subconscious mind, which is connected to our intuition, emotions, and vast storage of experience, takes in twenty million bits of data per second compared to our conscious mind, which will max out at forty bits. That's like a twenty-lane highway versus a single dirt track of processing speed and ability.

When you allow yourself to move from the day-to-day conscious mindset to access your subconscious, you are able to connect the dots that your conscious mind can't possibly hold. That's why intuition works so powerfully. Developmental biologist Bruce Lipton states, "The subconscious mind, the most powerful information processor known, specifically observes both the surrounding world and the body's internal awareness, reads the environmental cues, and immediately engages previously acquired (learned) behaviors—all without the help, supervision, or even awareness of the conscious mind."[10]

this in a mentoring debrief. When salespeople begin to track their own inner signals in a sales conversation, they can use this information to trust their guts in future conversations.

We can see how slowing down to connect with our intuition and access deeper nonconscious states can be implemented in a sales process with clear results, but this is equally true in other areas of decision-making in your business, such as strategic planning, product development, marketing, technology, hiring and recruiting, customer service, managing, and so much more. Jason Gore, cofounder and managing partner of Neuberg, Gore, and Associates, experiences this daily. Gore offers executive coaching to new generation CEOs and startups. He has seen the necessity of leaders slowing down from the over-adrenalized and over stimulated pressures of Silicon Valley, where they need to produce results *now* to warrant next rounds of funding, yet not lose track of the bigger picture of where they are leading their companies.

When I asked Jason how he gets business owners to tap into their deeper intuitive intelligence, he stated,

> *The first thing I do is get them to slow down and carve out time for strategy and big-picture thinking. Usually, they are spending a lot of time fighting fires, building operations, hiring, firing, etc. They're overly involved in every aspect of the business because they don't have a full team in place yet. When they carve out time in their calendar for uninterrupted strategic thinking, they can create a game plan and see the bigger picture. This gives them more room for creative flow, self-connection, and ultimately prioritizing the right things— rather than just drowning in day-to-day urgencies.[16]*

Being on the ground floor of Silicon Valley, Jason has seen the best innovative thinking happen when a leader goes against the impulse of longer hours and more production, and instead takes it down a notch to gain a wider perspective and strategy.

The Trifecta of Slowing Down

So what are the tools and methods of slowing down to listen to yourself or your team's deeper intelligence? The tool that works best will be personal to each team member and situation. There are three practices that you can integrate into your workspace that will have an immediate impact in slowing down, getting present, and accessing your team's deeper intuitive intelligence.

Stillness

In an increasingly fast-paced world, being still seems like a lost art. This is something that challenges me daily. I am addicted to the urge to be productive, hit all of my "to-dos," and get my dopamine rush. Yet when I make the time to stop, to be still, and to take a moment to come back into myself, my focus goes from narrow and pointed to wide and panoramic. My thoughts settle, and my breathing anchors me to the present moment. I relax. And even though it can be a daily fight to get there, once I'm still there's no more "getting there." I've arrived. In myself.

Once we are still, we can locate all of the movement, sensations, emotions, textures, feelings, and sounds that are going on inside of us all the time. And just like an animal tracker in the forest, we can also track movement outside of us in our environment, in our team meetings, or workstations.

Imagine you work for an up-and-coming media agency that is about to roll out new software that makes it easier for marketing managers to monitor the number of views and clicks on their team's latest ad campaigns, implementing the latest in AI. It's a mad scramble to the finish line as everyone knows competition is breathing down the agency's neck with similar state-of-the-art technology. This is your chance to help the business really get ahead. However, in the last project planning meeting, your fellow programmers doubt that they will finish on time and they won't have adequate space to beta test the software. And to top it off, they were getting pressure from the CEO (who was getting pressured from the board) to get this out there yesterday.

Amidst the anxiety and hustle of everyone trying to pull this off, you allow yourself to get quiet and still and drop into a reflective space in order to gather your thoughts. Right in the middle of the meeting, everyone starts to get quiet as they notice your sense of calmness. You stand out in the sea of chaos without even trying.

In that moment, it dawns on you that in the whirlwind of getting this software pushed out and getting carried away by the deadline, there needs to be some serious tweaks to the platform. Would you have the courage to speak from your gut sense? Postponing the launch would anger several stakeholders and people in the room, but in the long run would save money, time, and most importantly, the brand reputation.

I've seen courageous employees who are willing to speak up and risk the ire of those around them for what they are feeling and sensing deep inside. These are the moments that can make or break a company. No matter where you sit on the organizational chart, you have an opportunity to lead. When you allow yourself to get still amidst the chaos and listen to a deeper signal inside, it blazes the pathway and allows everyone else's nervous systems to also drop into a deeper place and help find a solution together.

Getting still allows us to come to our center and check in with ourselves on a deeper level. Once our internal background becomes still and clear, we notice what jumps out to us in the foreground. We observe the subtleties of our experience. We are no longer focused on the next shiny object outside of us or overly impacted by the vibes around us. This allows us to better track incongruencies and when something feels "off." Getting still can benefit you in any decision-making situation and will help you more accurately read the environment around you and within.

Silence

Silence is a rare yet powerful deviation from the typical business exchange. From top salespeople to negotiators, and from effective managers to customer service reps, silence helps you slow down, listen, and better understand the person in front of you in a deeper way. One of the most powerful techniques and ways of being that I learned in my own sales training, and the one that was the hardest for me to practice, was staying silent after asking a question.

There's a common tendency with salespeople, leaders, managers, and any technical experts, to fill the space with what they know, but that doesn't leave room to get underneath the needs and questions of the other person. You create a monologue, not a dialogue. And who likes to be talked at versus related to? This happens all the time in typical sales and leadership conversations.

Silence has a "pulling effect." When you ask a question and then create silence, it brings the other person out. There is a gravitational pull, and the other person has more space to share their real needs and wants. Yet, it is often difficult to be with the silence as it can bring up discomfort, social awkwardness, insecurities, and allows more space to feel things. When I used to do sales over the phone, I would duct tape my mouth after asking a question because I had such an impulse to ask a few questions in a row or answer my own question on behalf of the prospect. I wasn't comfortable with the silence, and I cringed when I heard my own sales recordings as I wasn't even aware how much this happened. Once I heard this, my relationships deepened and engagement increased. And not just in sales.

So many leaders, salespeople, technical experts, professors, and politicians want to fill the space with what they know, which is often a cover for an insecurity in relating. It is easier to over-rely on subject-matter content and not even realize that you just lost your audience. There's little to no room for engagement. Silence is the secret engager in a conversation. It leaves room for your intuition to guide you in what questions to ask next. This is where the relationship deepens.

Presence

When you practice slowing down, stillness, and silence, the net effect is more presence. You create a wide-angle lens that is able to take in more information. Just like in slow-motion instant replay, you can dissect the whole scene and get a better picture of what really happened. This is one of the greatest gifts you can give your team. The more you practice slowing down, the more you will stand out in a typically hectic workspace. And most importantly, you will be able to offer the timely insights and solutions that those around you missed, as you are now coming from a different perspective.

When you get more present in the moment, you create a more receptive space to listen to all of your signals and cues. You are now a notch deeper than the conscious mind and thoughts, and on the same resonance as intuition. Cultivating presence will help you in every facet of business, from more effective leadership and management, to understanding what makes your staff tick, to understanding the world of your customer, to improving partner relations, sales, networking, more effective hiring and recruiting, and hundreds of other applications. Plus, it just feels better to be present with yourself and your experience versus being disconnected and going a million miles a minute.

The key in the trifecta of slowing down is that you interrupt your normal thought stream. You slow down the process and allow space for your deeper subconscious and intuition to find you. There is no one-size-fits-all. Experiment and find out what works. If you stick with it as a regular practice, you will be amazed at some of the insights and awarenesses that you couldn't have reached with your conscious mind alone.

Slowing down can look like being still and not moving. It can look like meditation, slow walks in nature, and various mindfulness-based practices. Any type of relaxation activities like going to a sauna, going to a steam room, taking a hot shower, or getting a massage can help slow your thinking down and prove useful. Some of my best "aha" moments have come from these experiences. I've had visions for new trainings and things I wanted to teach that came to me in the steam room or shower. My hyperactive mind finally gets to settle down and I can naturally drop into a deeper awareness.

While not slowing down in the traditional sense, state changes are also effective because you shift gears into a new way of approaching a challenge. This is why leadership and team retreats can be so effective. You take yourself out of normal habits and office routines and are brought into a new environment that is conducive to deeper strategic thinking. You are more apt to get new ideas and inspirations as you have a fresh perspective in which to view a problem. The day-to-day distractions are gone and you can focus on the conversation with your full attention.

It also doesn't have to be so formal. If you are trying to work through a tough strategy or decision and can't seem to come up with a solution, you can simply use the time in your commute to turn off the radio, put down the phone, and tune into your inner state. From here you can ask a question and explore what your intuitive intelligence may be pointing you toward.

For others, exercising and getting into a flow state where the conscious mind isn't active can be the most helpful. Running, swimming, art, music, dance, yoga, martial arts, or other types of movement can bring about incredible insights as you are lost in the activity, which frees up aspects of your nonconscious mind. This allows new epiphanies to find you. The key is to find what works for you and then create space in your schedule where you or your team can get this strategic time. Slowing down is an action step. If you don't prioritize this, it won't happen.

Here's a simple mindfulness technique that you can use to help slow down, cultivate more presence, and connect with your innate intuitive intelligence.

Exercise: A Basic Mindfulness Technique

- Find a quiet space at home, in nature, in an empty conference room, or somewhere comfortable.

- Turn off all electronics, distractions, and anything that might interrupt you.

- Set a timer of how long you want to quiet your mind, so that you don't have to track the time.

- Once you are settled, tune into your breath. Simply follow the inhale and exhale in its full cycle and put your full attention here.

- Whenever any thoughts pop into your awareness, simply notice this and come back to your breathing in the present moment. Don't get hijacked by whatever thoughts you might have, which take you out of the present moment.

- Relax your gaze and let your whole body soften with each breath.

- There is no agenda but to slow down, breathe, and feel what you are feeling. From here you may notice certain sensations or inner signals that call your attention. Simply get curious and practice being in this receptive state with nothing to do or achieve. See what happens when you slow down and are open to what information might knock on the door of your awareness.

Conclusion

This second step of slowing down is critical to accessing your intuitive nature. Slowing down through practicing more moments of stillness, silence, and presence immediately expands your awareness to include your subconscious mind, so that you can integrate all the necessary data points in your decision-making. If you are anything like me and find slowing down a test, we now go to the most difficult challenge yet: dealing with our inner critic, who wants to take us out of our innate intelligence. Yet, this is the doorway we need to walk through to access our deeper states of being.

5

BEFRIEND YOUR INNER CRITIC

Looking back, my life seems like one long obstacle race, with me as its chief obstacle.

—Jack Paar

"Jonathan, this is what you do. You take too-big risks. You don't have a financial net here. You have a family. What are you going to do if this doesn't work?" he thought to himself. Jonathan Raymond[1] was staring at his bank account, hoping that he could will the numbers to change, but money wasn't coming in. The birth of his second daughter was only in a matter of weeks, and his anxiety was building. He followed his gut and launched his company Refound in 2015. Jonathan and his wife still believed in the radical direction that he had taken, but his new entrepreneurial vision wasn't manifesting.

Jonathan left his previous job, where he had a secure executive position, to follow the deeper calling that kept ringing deep inside. He had a strong intuition that he needed to embark on his own and create his own content and programs in the field of management consulting. He had tested and refined his methodologies about training managers and HR professionals in conducting the most effective one-to-ones possible. He knew that he had a fresh angle to contribute, which centered around helping companies and managers understand that employees thrive when their performances are connected to their personal growth and ambitions, and not keeping those two worlds separate.

When he published his first book on this topic, *Good Authority*, he hoped it would jump-start his career as he invested a lot of time and money in the production and launch. Although interest started to pique in his methodologies, it was far too quiet for his liking. His growing family didn't have the luxury of a financial safety net. He had to get traction soon and hope that HR departments nationwide understood the value of his material.

What made it even more challenging was the background noise of the inner critic in his head that stayed constant with each passing day. The messages ranged from, "You live in a small town and you don't have a network. You are not connected with people who could help you" to "Everyone's talking about being human at work and being your whole self. There's 30,000 books on leadership. Who the hell are you? You're just a guy." His inner critic was constant and using every doubt as ammunition to knock him down.

Jonathan had done years of personal development work and was no stranger to his inner critic. Yet, like many of us, when the risks are greater and stress mounts, it is easier to be taken over by this part of us. Jonathan was up against the perfect storm, which is when the inner critic tends to show up the strongest.

He had put on weight, second-guessed himself, and constantly questioned his decision to leave his secure job. He was competing with the gravitational pull of his inner critic and it was beginning to win. He was about to go on paternity leave for six weeks during his company's peak season, which didn't bode well for generating new business. Yet he knew that his family was his number-one priority and prayed that the rest would sort itself out.

After the next few days of really being "in it," he became more aware of how all-encompassing his inner critic's presence felt. This clued him into the fact that he had lost perspective. He remembered his personal development training that showed him how to track the characteristics of the critic's story and attitude versus his own. This gave him some space from his critic and he could breathe again as he was not consumed by the stress. Something inside of him relaxed on a deep level. He remembered that this was a *part* of him reacting, not all of who he is. When he wasn't feeding his doubts, he felt and trusted his inner radar and knew he was on the right path.

And although Jonathan had some naysayers around him, his wife and close friends were incredibly supportive and helped strengthen the belief that he had in himself. He had previous experience trusting his gut during some big life decisions and it had always served him, even when the ride was not comfortable. This was one of those moments.

At the time, a webinar that he led for an HR company exploded in popularity, and he was attracting interest on a level that he had never seen before. This translated into clients who were hungry for the trainings and consulting he offered. The voice of his inner critic had quieted down as the conviction in his inner compass grew louder and louder. His recent outward success confirmed that his work in separating the voice of his intuition from the voice of his inner critic was making the difference.

With each passing day, he made a choice to listen to the kernel of cautionary wisdom from his inner critic, yet not let this become his whole reality. He instead put his attention on his passions and building more content, value, and creating the relationships that aligned with his work. He was able to recognize and tune out the old tapes of doubt and fear playing in his head. With each subsequent win, he was able to build momentum toward his goals.

A year or so later, he was hiring and expanding faster than expected. He even had to get more selective in what opportunities the company took on. He attributes this to his willingness to stick it out and trust his inner guidance, especially when the doubters on the outside and the ones on the inside wouldn't subside. Facing this challenging career moment and moving through it head-on emboldened him to base future risk-taking on how much he felt connected to his gut sense underneath all of the noise. His relationship strengthened with his inner compass and became a trustable resource for decision-making and future success.

Once we begin to slow down and focus our attention inward, we may realize how noisy we actually are on the inside. As Jonathan's story demonstrates, one of the biggest obstacles that we have to living from our intuitive center is our inner critic. The third step focuses on how to separate from the voice of the inner critic. We have so much programming and messages that we've taken in from the outside world, starting from childhood, that we often don't even recognize our own inner voice. When we make allies with our inner critic, we can eliminate doubts and distraction and find alignment with a deeper place inside of us. Once the critic is no longer an impediment, more room and space open up for self-discovery and our intuitive intelligence, which is the birthplace of innovation.

What Is the Inner Critic?

The inner critic is the critical voice inside your head. It is a broken record of the same stories and themes that you've been hearing most of your life. These old tape recordings are one of the tell-tale signs that your inner critic is active. It has a false confidence that knows how everything will play out, based on past judgements, stereotypes, opinions, and criticisms. It's a lens of the past that you see your current reality through if you don't get enough separation from it.

It usually comes in three distinct themes: You are not good enough, you are doing something wrong, or it constantly compares you to others. It's the part of you that is never satisfied and judges you and others with the conclusion that ultimately you are never enough, or that you are too much.

And as in life, this shows up in business all the time and gets in the way of confidence, performance, and success. "I can never get ahead." "Everyone does it better than me." "I hope no one sees that I don't know what I'm doing." "I don't think they really like me." "I never get the credit I deserve." "I can't trust other people." These are all common examples of the different narratives commonly referred to as imposter syndrome[2] that are running in the back of our minds at work. Whatever position we hold on the organizational chart, our critic will find ways to minimize our contributions and potential, or over inflate them. The net result of these negative beliefs is that you feel like a fraud, you'll get "found out," and you'll never accept yourself as you are.

In Chapter 2, we looked at the five obstacles of intuition. And although I write "obstacles," there is not something "out there" that gets in our way. When we fall into one of these five ruts, we often become our own worst enemy as we unconsciously allow a part of us to sabotage our success. And although each obstacle has its own challenges that prevent us from connecting with and living from our intuitive intelligence, the inner critic, which uses doubt as its favorite weapon, is probably the most crippling.

My relationship to my inner critic has shifted from not being aware of it to running away from it, avoiding it, projecting it on others, fighting and judging it, and finally getting into a relationship with it and integrating this core aspect of myself. One of my main aims in life has been to find a sense of inner peace as I never had it, no matter what my life looked like on the outside.

If left unchecked, the inner critic impedes us from listening to our intuitive intelligence and thwarts our success at work more than any external factor. If you can learn how to work with your inner critic, understand its positive intention, and integrate its wisdom but not let it hijack your perspective, you will be more integrated and effective at work and beyond. The shift happens when you realize that it is serving a function for you or it wouldn't exist. It is protecting you from getting hurt again. Instead of blaming the inner critic, learn to understand the motives and befriend this very part of you that you may constantly battle. That is how integration happens.

Differentiate the Voice of the Inner Critic from the Voice of Your Intuition

How do you distinguish your inner critic's voice from the voice of your intuition? The inner critic is a stream of thoughts that can only live in the past or the future. It can never be in the present, which is exactly where the voice of your intuition lives. Because of this, the inner critic is reactive. It is reacting to your current situation based on outdated information, and then also projecting this into the future. It distorts your perspective using a past experience of you to navigate the present moment. This happens all the time in business as it's easy to default to old habits and patterns that have worked previously. Problems occur when we stop bringing a fresh perspective to current challenges and overlay what worked in the past onto the current landscape. The inner critic tries to protect you from repeating mistakes, failures, or something painful that you experienced, even an embarrassing or insecure moment. It will scan future moments to avoid this possibility at all costs. Its job is to keep things familiar and predictable so that it can stay in control.

Understanding the critic's motivation is vital, as its goal is not in learning, innovating, risk-taking, and aliveness. "The mind and the inner critic's orientation has one purpose: safety and security. If you are trying to create safety, security, predictability, and comfort, then listening to your inner critic may produce that outcome,"[3] says Mesha Joy Machamer, a psychotherapist, supervisor, and consultant to business executives. "But if you want to be successful in business and feel your greatest aliveness every day as you evolve and innovate, leaders need to learn to listen to their intuition. People

DIFFERENTIATE THE VOICE OF THE INNER CRITIC AND YOUR INTUITION

	Inner Critic	Intuition
Time:	Past/Future	Present
Behavior:	Reactive	Responsive
Action:	Pushing/Forcing	Receiving
Orientation:	Safety/Security	Aliveness/Openness
Tone:	Dark/Heavy/ Negative/Dramatic	Clear/Light/Drama-free
Perception:	Judge	Discern
Emotions:	Guilt/Shame/Fear/ Insecurity/Dread/ Paranoia	Reassurance/Peace/ Excitement/Warmth

Figure 2.

will pay attention when they sense you are following something alive as opposed to something predictable. It's contagious."[4]

The voice of your intuition is alive, responsive, and adaptable, as it's not weighed down by the baggage of the past. This allows for a more objective view and accurate relationship of what's happening in the moment, as well as anticipation of what needs to happen next. Business leaders who can separate the voice of their critic from their intuition accelerate faster than those who can't.

The voice of the inner critic is usually more dramatic, heavy, critical, negative, and darker. It is often accompanied by feelings of guilt, shame, insecurity, dread, fear, and paranoia. The voice of your intuition is drama-free. It is clear and light, and there's a sense of something that adds up or feels right, without all the extra emotional charge. You enter the world of potential and new possibilities.

The Inner Critic and the Self

In my fifteen years as a coach and consultant, I can say without hesitation that a business owner's or manager's inner critic is the number-one saboteur to his or her growth and success. It is the main reason that leaders don't trust their gut intuition, are too worried about what other people think, and get in their own way. It can manifest as constant self-doubt, not taking action steps, worst-case scenario-izing, avoiding confrontation, being overly critical of everyone around you, micromanaging staff, seeking perfection, always looking over your shoulder, and ultimately never being satisfied nor finding a state of inner peace. Even if you are successful by everyone else's metrics!

The inability to accept flaws and mistakes, or having the belief that we are bad, creates an internal split because we want to distance ourselves from the part of us that we are ashamed of. The problem then gets compounded when we project our reality onto everyone around us. If I'm on high alert and fearful of losing my job, my inner critic will constantly look for evidence around me, and assume any gesture or behavior is a sign that he (or she) is right. In other words, inner critics live in a world of confirmation bias where they are always looking to selectively confirm their reality and then miss all of the other data in the environment.

Our relationship with our self is the most intimate relationship we'll ever know, and the one we often avoid. By looking closer at this dynamic, we can make the biggest gains in our professional and personal lives. This comes from getting into more relationships with our inner critic, not less. "You have to have a relationship to your inner critic, or everybody else in your company will have to," says Mesha Joy. "If you are avoiding that conversation within yourself, it will impact everyone around you. People tend to think that the inner critic is between them and themselves in a silo, but it's not. It's playing out all the time in how you perceive relationships and inhabit your role as a leader."[5]

The inner critic has been our background noise for so long that most of us are unaware of it and simply assume its narrative is true. If you were a fish, it would be the water that you swim in. Even more destructively, you assume this voice is your own. In other words, you often don't question this voice and assume its reality *is* reality.

How the Inner Critic Is Formed

The inner critic is made up of our internalized messaging and conditioning that we swallowed growing up, based on the judgements, projections, and expectations of those around us. We didn't have a mechanism developed as children that could discern what was true for us and what wasn't. The critic's voice is usually a combination of previous authorities, often our parents, but could be anyone of significant influence who we looked up to, respected, or who we were wary of. In addition to parental messaging, the inner critic is also formed by all of the messages we take in from our religions, cultures, mentors, teachers, peers, media, and various authorities that try to tell us who we are and how we should be. Researcher and cell biologist Bruce Lipton states, "Once we accept the perceptions of others as 'truths,' *their* perceptions become hardwired into our own brains, becoming *our* 'truths.'"[6] The real damage accumulates when we mistake the critic's narrative for our own.

The inner critic forms around our core negative beliefs such as: "I'm not enough," "I will never get (love, attention, respect, validation)," "I am not (good looking, strong, slim, smart, creative, confident) enough," "I'm too needy," "I'm not wanted," and so on. On the flipside, our critic can also form around grandiosity and thinking that we are better than everyone else, which still keeps us in a loop of comparison and insecurity. We all have our own signature wound pattern that formed in childhood, which represents our unique version of unworthiness. If we don't identify it and get into a relationship with our own particular lack shape and its tendencies, then it can take over who we are, how we relate with others, and how we live our lives. Before we know it, we are operating our lives from this place, yet trying desperately to not let others see these vulnerable parts of ourselves.

The Inner Critic at Work

How does this dynamic show up in business? As the adage goes, "How we do anything is how we do everything." How you show up and interact in business is a reflection of your deeply held beliefs about yourself and the world. On one hand, if you were raised to believe that life is fair, everyone has opportunity, and you always have a chance to rise up in any given situation, you will perform in a way that is aligned with those beliefs. On the other hand, if you were raised to believe that you can't trust other people and everyone is out to get you, this will show up as well, no matter what role you play in your company or whatever situation you find yourself in. If you don't do your inner work to identify your patterns, they will unconsciously run the show.

The critic will often take on the voice of your manager or supervisor. We tend to project our past wounds from previous authority figures onto our new ones. Over time, we might find ourselves acting very differently in front of our boss (or if you are the CEO, your board of directors). We might try to hide a mistake that we made, or what we don't know, or overcompensate in the other direction to win our supervisor's approval.

I once was hired as a business coach for a company and became very comfortable within this role. I had a set schedule, benefits, didn't have to find clients, and simply got to coach. It was a great job, yet after some time, they changed their business model, and I was asked to become an independent contractor instead of an employee.

At first I was flooded with doubts that I could make it on my own; I had grown accustomed to the perks of having a job, and in some ways, being taken care of. I had started two other businesses previously, so I knew I could do it, but it seemed like a large task to all of a sudden deal with my own website, accounting, marketing, sales, and launching my brand of coaching. My inner critic jumped at the opportunity to pound on me, and I felt a lot of fear during the transition. "What if I can't get my own clients? What if this doesn't work? What if I'm a business coach who can't run his own business? Am I a fraud? I guess I'll scoop ice cream as a backup plan." (Yes, my inner critic actually said this. Somehow that's always his last resort.)

After being fused to my critic for a couple of days and feeling overwhelmed, I started to notice all of the negative thinking that was swirling around in my head. I realized this was the part of me that was just scared of change. And although my critic had doubts about my capabilities, I knew that I had done this before and I knew how to develop a business. I then had more room to get excited about what I wanted to create. That's when something moved through me that I had never felt as an employee. I felt the entrepreneurial fever and had the opportunity to create the business I always wanted.

I wrote down all of the steps needed to start up a new business, just like how I coach my clients. I also had the help of a fellow coach who was launching his own business at the same time, and who became an accountability partner. We met at our local coffee shop weekly and reviewed how we were going to move our businesses forward that next week. I felt on-task and became incredibly passionate in the coming weeks and months. Nothing was going to stop me, not even my critic.

I doubled my revenue that first year upon leaving the company, traveled the world leading trainings, and had more fun working with businesses than I ever imagined. It wasn't always easy and I worked my butt off. But I was committed to creating a business that I loved. Recognizing that I was fused to my inner critic and getting some separation from this part of me made all the difference. I then had room to listen to my intuition regarding what I wanted to create and what I needed to do to make it happen.

Make Friends with Your Inner Critic

The following is an effective system I have used to work with the inner critic if it comes up in your professional world. This is a synthesis of the best modalities that I've learned throughout my years as a therapist, coach, and mentor in working with people from all walks of life. It is meant to be a practical tool that you can use in the heat of the moment at work, or in the middle of an unproductive habit that you want to change. And for our purposes, working with the critic in this way will make more room for your intuitive voice to show up at work and lead. If you put the following exercise to the test and feel like you are not gaining traction, you might want to consider further exploration with a professional in your network.

Five Steps to Befriend Your Inner Critic

1. Map Your Critic's Shape

The first step is about detecting the "shape" of your inner critic. The key distinction is that the inner critic is a part of you, it's not all of you. This statement changes everything. It's the part of you that's primarily concerned with your safety and security. The more you understand its characteristics and attitudes through stories, themes, behaviors, moods, emotions, textures, flavors, colors, and how it feels in your body physically, you will start to identify how this *aspect* of you is different than *you*. This will give you more breathing space and allow you the ability to listen to your own deeper nature and others without background interference.

Think about a time when you were challenging yourself at work. Perhaps you were leading a team for the first time, or learning a new skill that you had to implement. The inner critic often shows up when you grow into new territories because there is something at risk. You may have heard some version of "I can't do this. This isn't going to work out. People will see that I don't know what I am doing."

You might remember that your whole mood, posture, and perspective changed when the inner critic took over. Especially when you took its reality as yours. The key in this first step is to identify how your critic tends to show up. The more you track its shape, the more you can create separation. It's usually a broken record of the same thoughts and feelings that crop up from time to time. It will be very familiar to you.

If you want to put these steps into practice, write down the following categories: voice and messages, moods and emotions, behaviors, and body language. Now bring to mind the last time you felt bombarded by your critic who was either making you wrong, telling you that you weren't enough, or comparing you to others. Being able to imagine these moments and sense what it's like when the critic is running the show is key. Don't censor yourself and write down whatever comes to you when you tune into the inner critic's narrative.

2. Separate the Part from the Whole

Once you get the flavor, colors, and shape of your inner critic, you start to get its overall impression. This will help in detecting when it's activated. The next step is about naming the inner critic as only a part of you, when it's present. This may seem like a simple step, but it goes a long way in extricating yourself from the critic. By naming the critic as a "part of you" when it's active, you immediately create separation, as you are getting perspective from its reality. On the contrary, when you are fused to it, you *are* it.

The old adage states that if you can name it, you can tame it. If you can start to recognize the pattern of what is happening, then you are by definition not submersed in it anymore. You can then start to shift your orientation. I find it really helpful to use humor and lightness with this process when possible as it's not meant to be a heavy, loaded, examination of self. Critic material is already so heavy that often bringing levity can help balance it all out. For example, "Oh, there's my inner critic again!" or "Apparently, my inner critic thinks that I shouldn't be the one to do the investment pitch," as you smile in its attempt to thwart you.

This is where humor is the great differentiator as it helps loosen the grip of the critic's reality. If I'm working with a business owner and their critic is strongly present, I'll sometimes name this in a direct, yet teasing or playful way. This lets my clients know not to take their critic's point of view so seriously. In other words, if I'm not fooled by the critic's narrative and have freedom to be playful and flexible, so can my client.

You can practice by saying statements out loud, such as, "The part of me that thinks our customers always complain wants to ignore them. But we are going to do the opposite and reach out right now." This is the beginning of taking your power back versus handing it over to this part of you. You then make room for your own self-leadership to emerge and the voice of your innate intuition and intelligence.

Now that you've written down its identifiers, the next step is to name when your inner critic is present. In the act of labelling it, you create separation. For one client, "doom and gloom" worked because it was so opposite of his true nature that it really helped him get an edge on this part of him. For others, simply naming it as a part of you or as "my inner critic" will help you get perspective right away. Doing this out loud for yourself or with others around can also help diffuse the critic's hold on you.

3. Get the Positive Intention

The next step is to understand the positive intention of what the critic wants for you in the moment. It's your job to make room for that intelligence and learn why and what it's protecting. Then you can understand its function and begin to integrate its wisdom, versus banishing this part of you and continually being at war with yourself. When you can accept how it's trying to serve you, the critic begins to disarm its grip. There is nothing to fight because you are both on the same side. When you befriend this part of you, you start the integration process and move toward wholeness.

You can ask your critic what it's been protecting. You'll be surprised at the logic and wisdom of its response. You can simply ask what it wants right now. How is it trying to serve you? What's at risk if you follow through with the behavior you are being warned about? For example, you might find out that the critic is trying to prevent you from repeating a past experience in which you trusted someone and felt betrayed, or a time when you delegated work to someone else and you felt let down. When you bring your curiosity to the critic and begin to understand and empathize with what it's trying to protect, it will start to relax and you might feel the vulnerability underneath.

4. Restore Self-Leadership

Once you get separation from the critic and understand its positive intention of why it's trying to protect you, you will notice a feeling that comes with its story. For example, you might feel the hurt that comes from being deceived by a previous director, and that now makes you distrust other authorities. Getting underneath the story and accepting this feeling is key to integration. "If you can feel that feeling and accept it, then you are present with the feeling, and allowing it to be what it is," says Mesha Joy. "Just that very act of allowing a feeling to be what it is, without attempting to change it, you have taken a significant step towards becoming the leader of yourself and taking over the job that your inner critic thinks it needs to do. It's a changing of the guard."[7]

Once you are able to get the feeling, even if you don't know what it is, simply let yourself feel it and accept it. Don't push it away. The more you let this feeling be, the inner critic no longer has a job to do as you are now on it. Embrace the shame, guilt, anger, grief, disappointment, fear, or whatever feeling is underneath the critic's story, and you will learn that you can feel it directly and it doesn't kill you. You can learn to tolerate anything that you feel. This is how you begin to restore trust and repair your reputation with yourself.

The ability to feel is enough to keep you in the present moment and not circling in your thoughts about the past. From this place, you can respond from your intuitive resilience that's not reacting from old wound narratives. You become the advocate for yourself in a way that you could not have possibly been as a child. The critic no longer needs to take over as watchdog. Your self-leadership shines forth, and you are no longer hijacked by stories from the past because you can now see the current situation more clearly. This is where self-acceptance leads to wholeness, as you and your critic finally get that you are on the same side, and that its services are no longer required.

Working with your inner critic is a life long practice. Sometimes it's enough to feel these feelings and get that it's been going on for a while, and accepting this is enough. Other times it persists and there is something more meaningful and powerful about getting more assistance. Part of self-leadership is recognizing when you need a little more help, and this can be a powerful way to build more self-awareness and integration. Trust your intuition regarding what your needs are in your situation, and seek out a supportive practitioner near you if you are curious to follow up.

Practice locating the emotion that the critic's story is attached to. Even if you don't know what emotion it is, try to stay with the feeling and accept this part of you that the critic is protecting. The more that you can feel it, accept it, and be present with it, the quicker the critic will disarm and relax. You are stepping into your self-leadership.

5. Opposite Action Steps

When your inner critic experiences that you are "home" and it no longer needs to protect you from being hurt or making mistakes, trust is restored. This trust is built on accepting and feeling what the critic is protecting. Performing an opposite action step of its narrative really encourages the change of you leading instead of your critic. It is another layer of differentiation. You wire new neural pathways that establish updated ways of being, which are more integrated and whole. The moment that you do something different, you know it is possible. You've now stepped into that potential. The critic's story that you "can't" no longer holds any weight.

"If you could see fifty times where you were incongruent with yourself and how that resulted in outcomes that didn't serve you, this would provide momentum to try something different," says Mesha Joy. "But often times, leaders don't see the root of the repetition and need to actually try something different to illuminate the issue. These steps are not against the critic, rather actions that help you experience more of who you are. When you take steps to do something different, you start to experience new outcomes that were otherwise invisible."[8] In other words, this is progress in action.

For example, I have worked with several business owners who say that they want feedback about their leadership from their team, but the inner critic prevents this from happening. In many of these cases, feedback was seen as an attack by the critic, and these opportunities never happened. Employees would not approach these leaders after meetings because they could sense that this person was not really welcoming feedback on a deeper level.

With one such client, we worked on this dynamic for a while, and he eventually saw how he was sending mixed messages: He said he wanted feedback, but then he tracked how this part of him saw feedback as criticism that he was doing something wrong. We took gradual steps to reframe what feedback was really about, and he was able to accept the part of himself that gets scared around making potential mistakes and not being perfect, which was what he was criticized for throughout his childhood. The opposite action step was to get curious about other people's experience of his leadership in one-on-one settings. He was able to receive this and not let his critic hijack the process.

The grand finale was when he wanted to do a 360-degree assessment on his leadership with his whole team—when he was not in the room. When I wrapped up this process with his team, he was genuinely excited to hear the feedback and had moved beyond the old stories of criticism and doing things imperfectly that held him back for so long. Because of this, his self-leadership grew as others could contribute to his development.

What is an opposite action step that you can take that would go against the narrative of your inner critic, so that you can experience more of you? If your inner critic procrastinates, start working on that task right now. If your critic blames others on your team for mistakes, what can you take ownership of proactively? If there's a lot of hesitation and dread in leading a training, how can you practice leaning into it? When you practice these new behaviors, you are wiring new neural pathways and setting the foundation for leading in a new way that honors your self-leadership.

Conclusion

Distinguishing our intuitive voice from the voice of our inner critic is the third step in our series and a massive step in leading from our true nature. Having access to this resource allows for more adaptability, intelligent responsiveness, and innovation. These five steps of befriending your inner critic are essential for success in business and will have immediate impact if you make the time to disidentify with its reality and integrate it into your whole self. By getting into a relationship with this part of you, you no longer give your power away through constant power struggles. Now you have space and more peace to listen to the wisdom of your body, which is our fourth step, and exactly where the deeper voice and messaging of your intuition awaits you.

Your Body Is Wiser than Your Mind

6

Our body knows things the mind does not have access to.

—Marcel Marceau

Deborah Bowman[1] awoke that cold morning in September. She didn't want to leave her sleeping bag and venture out of her tent; her body knew she should still be sleeping. She huddled one more time in the warmth of her cocoon before she needed to get up. She was on a climbing expedition with a small group of instructors from NOLS and Outward Bound in the Wind River Range of Wyoming. They were out in the wilderness to spend a week together climbing in the high mountains. She worked at NOLS as an assistant to instructors on basic wilderness courses, but had never ice climbed before. Deborah had experience leading on easier rock climbs and had only experienced ice climbing through rappelling into crevasses and climbing out with the protection of an overhead rope. She knew how to traverse glaciers, stop herself from falling (known as a "self-arrest"), and how to rescue someone who had fallen into a crevasse. She had no experience leading on a mountain wall of ice.

Deborah hiked twenty-three miles into the mountains with an eighty-pound pack the day before and then the group divided into teams of two to ascend various walls in the area. She prepared to follow the lead of another member of the team on an ice climb at dawn. On top of the usual nerves from being outside her comfort zone, she was not at full strength. Her balance was not 100 percent, as she was recovering from a serious bout of mononucleosis and was still on meds. Regardless, she decided to take part in the climb. Being this immersed in nature hit her on a deep, spiritual level, and she wanted to participate in all of it.

This was the 1970s, and the mountaineering culture at the time was very male-dominated as women were just getting into the sport. The mottos were "Just push through!" and "Go for it!" Deborah's family also taught her to "be the good girl" and to just say yes all the time. "No" was not part of her vocabulary. She was excited by the challenge of testing her physical limits and exploring the world of ice climbing, yet her body was trying to speak to her.

To top it off, she learned the day before that the man she used to date, who was also in this small group of instructors, was now pursuing one of the other women in their group. Deborah was upset, but tried to push this down along with all of her other feelings in order to stay on-target with the mission. She had the mindset that when you are out in the wilderness doing demanding activities, you have to turn some things off mentally so you can get into gear. This was part of her conditioning as a girl, as she had an immense willpower to push through when necessary.

After getting up and having some hot oatmeal and coffee with the group, they started to plan for climbing and paired off. A man from the group asked her to partner on an ice wall. Deborah said yes, even though she barely knew him. In fact, she had just met him at the trailhead the day before. They gathered their gear and went to the base of the climb. Her heart was pounding—in hindsight her body was telling her no, but she wasn't able to listen. She spent twenty-seven years being numbed out and out of touch with her feelings. Her family strategy was to pretend that everything was okay and muscle through adversity. Today was no different.

As she looked up, some of the climbing terrain looked easy, and some of it felt daunting. Deborah and her partner made small conversation and started playing around with their tools in the ice. Deborah knew that she could look like she knew what she was doing, even when she didn't. She practiced going up and down four to five feet to test the ice and her tools.

Her climbing partner went up first and ascended a couple hundred feet. She waited by the base and felt numbness throughout her body. That's when she heard the clarion call from above that startled her: "Bring up the rope!" She mobilized into action and started her ascent.

The first section looked reasonable, she thought to herself. It was still a little bit out of her league, but she was in motion nonetheless. Deborah climbed most of the way up, but then got to a juncture where it became increasingly steep just below where her partner was located. She also realized that the snow had changed. It was no longer the grabby frozen snow. It was ice.

She wondered how she was going to get over to her climbing partner. The problem is, if you put your ice axe into hard ice, the ice can shatter instead of grabbing in. With frozen snow, it's safe. But ice makes it hard to find placement with your tools.

Deborah decided that it was too much to make it to where he was. She looked for an alternative and found a potential anchor point five or six feet above him. It was at an angle that wasn't directly in line with him, which would be dangerous. She had to navigate three feet of ice to get there. This was her best option.

Without taking a moment to check in with herself, she attempted to cross the crystal blue surface. The ice axe didn't stick. She looked over and saw him for an instant and then started to fall. Everything was whizzing by as she descended away from the ice wall. As soon as she started free falling, a natural intelligence started to kick in.

She had taken an avalanche course from an instructor who had fallen 1,000 feet and survived. His words reverberated in her mind as she started falling: "Stay upright." If not, she could easily tumble backward and break her back or get seriously injured.

The slope was fairly steep and, although everything whizzed by, she noticed every detail as if she was in slow motion. She remembered the self-arrest posture where you stick your elbows and knees into the surface to slow down. You don't want to use your axe or crampons because your foot can catch while the rest of you goes backward.

As she slid down in the correct self-arrest posture, the slope was becoming less steep. Deborah was still falling at a high velocity when one of her crampons caught in the snow debris and spun her around. She stopped suddenly and her whole body whiplashed like a spring and then came back. She was just sitting there, heart pounding, taking in the view and feeling overwhelming gratitude for being alive. The view was breathtaking.

When the crampon caught and she boomeranged out, the stress of that impact pulled her ankle out of joint and dislocated it. She felt no pain with the endorphin rush as she looked out at the spell-binding landscape. She also realized that she could only see out of one eye. Deborah decided not to worry about that in the moment and just focused on getting down safely. Eventually, her climbing partner found his way to her and miraculously another hiker happened to be in the area, which was deep in the backcountry. They worked together to lower Deborah down several hundred feet, taking almost seven rope lengths.

She made it back to camp and was comforted with just a couple of aspirin. She never lost lucidity and was barely aware of the shock or trauma moving through her body. This was the days before cell phones, and it was twenty-three miles back to the trailhead. Immediately, two members of the expedition volunteered to walk out with headlamps in the dark to get help and managed to find a phone booth by dawn. By late morning, a rescue helicopter arrived to escort her to the hospital.

Later that day, she learned that the vision loss in her injured eye was permanent and would later have it removed to avoid infecting the good eye.[2] There was some black-studded ice that she hit on the way down, and it left granite in the eye.

While this turned out to be an immensely painful lesson on the price of not trusting her own intuition, Deborah did not let this stop her. It took her several years to fully realize how disconnected she had been from her body and her feelings. This understanding started a new pathway forward in life that would have her work through the trauma, enjoy the outdoors in new ways, and help others heal as well. She eventually became a renowned psychotherapist, founder of Transpersonal Counseling Psychology and Wilderness Therapy programs, as well as Dean at Naropa University.

In hindsight, she identified all the places where she felt hesitation and where her nervous system and body were warning her to not move forward with the climb: Being sick, dealing with her ex-boyfriend flirting with another woman, being aware that she was outside of her skill set when she started the climb, bringing up the rope, and trying to get to her climbing partner were all moments that she now recognizes as her body and her intuition speaking to her very clearly. She now is able to listen to and track those inner nuances and help bring this learning to others in her work and teaching.

I asked Deborah if she took any meaning from losing her eye during this incident. Without missing a beat, she said:

I was blind to myself. I was blind to the world. I was blind to people's intentions and people's ignorance. And my own ignorance. I had been taught to just pretend that some of the warning signs that I sensed in others weren't there. To help make people feel good. My body knew better, but I wasn't quite connected to it. Now I am. Now I listen to my intuition a whole lot more.[3]

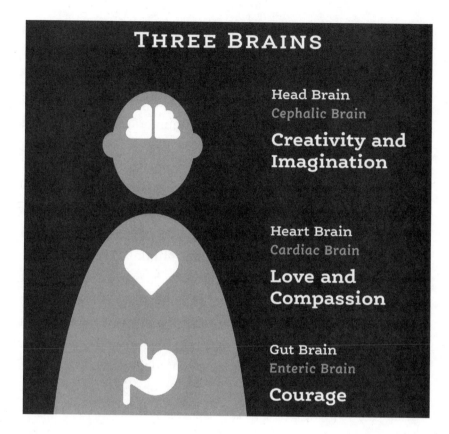

Figure 3.

The Three Brains

How common is this for us? How often is the wisdom of your body speaking to you throughout the day, when you feel a strong or subtle affirmation or hesitation, and you are not listening to these signals and cues? Many of us are stuck in our mental loops and narratives, oblivious to all of the data around us and inside of us. That's why listening to the body is our fourth step. It is a distinct advantage in business and in life, as we are open to more data that's available to us all the time for a more well-rounded perspective. This is the secret to making better decisions, and at faster rates.

Yet we live in an era where we still worship the mind. We worship empirical evidence, science, facts, numerics, reasoning, and logic. There is a rightful place for these more objective metrics. The problem occurs when we create a strong bias toward these approaches and minimize other mediums of data and intelligence. According to Grant Soosalu and Marvin Oka, who compiled research on bringing a whole-body approach to decision-making in accessing our nonconscious mind and intuition, "If we can't explain something in head-based objective terms, we denigrate it or ignore it."[4] Our perspectives become imbalanced and we miss out on a more holistic picture. Although empirical evidence has its place and can make the world seem more safe and predictable, the reality is that there is a chaotic element to life that we can never fit inside a formula or spreadsheet. This is why opening up to the wisdom of the body is so crucial.

One of the most exciting revelations in neuroscience in the last twenty-five years has been the research and discovery that we actually have three brains, not just one! Brains are made up of neurons, ganglia, and a storage of neurotransmitters, which act as a network to process and assimilate information, store and access memory, and direct and manage our nervous system, reflexes, and sensory and motor activities. We actually have neural networks in the gut, the heart, and the head, which have their own command centers and intelligence (see Figure 3). There have been more studies done on how these three brains communicate and interact with each other for optimal human functioning.[5] The following is a summary of these command centers, based on the works of Soosalu and Oka in their outstanding book, *mBraining.*

The Heart Brain

In 1991, Dr. J. Andrew Armour[6] discovered that the heart (cardiac brain) has a complex intrinsic nervous system that qualifies as a brain. There are somewhere between 40,000 and 120,000 neurons in the heart brain. In some cases, it can "function independently of the head brain and it can learn, remember, feel and sense."[7] It can also grow new neurons and make new neural connections. It can learn, adapt, and change. It secretes hormones such as dopamine and norepinephrine (which were previously thought to only exist in the head brain), and oxytocin, which is the love or bonding hormone, and responsible for our social cues, adaptation, and what I call "social intuition."

In fact, the HeartMath Institute (*www.heartmath.org*) was founded upon these principles and has done a lot of research to prove the intelligence of the heart in its own right. The heart also sends messages to the brain that affect our behavior. It's a two-way street as these neural centers work together. The primary function of the heart brain involves love, care, desires, intimacy, connection, affection, passion, kindness, goals, dreams, and values. The heart can be summed up as the expression of love and compassion.

The Gut Brain

The gut brain, also known as the enteric brain, is considered our oldest and most primordial brain, and really came into our recent cultural awareness with Dr. Michael Gershon's book, *The Second*

Brain: Your Gut Has a Mind of Its Own.[8] "The gut can work independently of any control by the brain in your head—it's functioning as a second brain," says Gershon.[9] The gut brain was actually discovered more than one hundred years ago but got lost in the shuffle. In 1907, Byron Robinson wrote *The Abdominal And Pelvic Brain,*[10] which referenced some of these same connections, yet for reasons unknown, the medical field left this knowledge behind. We have more than 500 million neurons in our gut, which is equivalent to the size of a cat's brain. It also contains every class of neurotransmitters found in the head brain, which is the other brain Gershon refers to in his book. The gut can also learn, adapt, and can form memories of its own. "Developmentally, the gut brain forms first in nature and in the womb, followed by the heart and then the head brains."[11]

The main functions of the gut brain involve protection, self-preservation, mobility, willpower, and core identity. Soosalu and Oka make the case that back when evolution was comprised of amoebas and simple organisms, the gut brain was the only developed one. Its objective was to move away from danger and move toward food. Times have not changed much as we still operate from these basic drivers, no matter how sophisticated we see ourselves. In the business world, moving away from perceived threats and toward rewards are what drive salespeople, leaders, marketers, managers, and motivated staff across all departments. The gut brain "is expressed as motivation, gutsy courage, and a gut-felt desire to take action (or not)."[12]

The Head Brain

The head brain, also known as the cephalic brain, is the largest and most complex neural network with more than eighty-six billion

136

neurons. It is involved in all functions on some level. The main job of the head brain is to process information, make sense of the world, and provide executive control. It mediates complex reflexes through our nervous system and it also involves logical thinking, reasoning, perception, mental imagery, abstraction, language expression, and deciphering meaning. It's ultimately about creativity in the highest expression and function.

Right Brain Versus Left Brain

The head brain is divided into two hemispheres. For more than a century, we've known that the brain's two sides serve different functions. "Accidents, strokes, and tumors in the left hemisphere generally impair activities of the rational, verbal, nonintuitive mind, such as reading, writing, speaking, arithmetic reasoning, and understanding,"[13] says social psychologist David Myers, in his book *Intuition*. "The right brain is superior to the left at copying drawings, recognizing faces, perceiving differences, sensing and expressing emotion. Although the left brain is adept at literal interpretations of language, the right brain excels in making subtle inferences."[14] Integrating the two sides of the brain has powerful implications because our social intuition, which is associated with the more intuitive right side of the brain, compliments the logical facts that we are observing from the left side of the brain. In tandem, we can make better decisions at work and beyond.

Perhaps the battle for superiority between both sides of the brain can finally end, as Gerard P. Hodgkinson and his team of researchers have been discovering.[15] Hodgkinson considers this an outmoded view as modern research shows how both sides of the brain work together in parallel process. Recent advances in cognitive and social cognitive neuroscience have displaced the notion that individuals are marked by an overwhelming preference for analytical or intuitive approaches to information processing, a tendency historically attributed to gross hemispheric specialization.[16] In other words, as we have put our focus of study on each hemisphere of the brain, we have forgotten to "zoom out" and understand the interconnectedness of how the hemispheres actually work together for greater decision-making. "Skilled strategic decision-making requires the blending of intuitive and analytic approaches to information processing in ways that enable the decision-making unit, whether an individual, group or multiple groups, to appreciate important details, while also maintaining a bigger picture."[17]

The Wisdom in Our Cells

Lastly, in *Molecules of Emotion,* Candace Pert discovered that neural receptors were present in most, if not all of the body's cells.[18] The mind is not just concentrated in the head, but distributed throughout the body through the signal molecules of our neural network. And while the conscious mind is mostly located in the head brain, we severely limit ourselves if we are not open to accessing our subconscious and unconscious, which is found throughout the cells in our body. This is why heart wisdom, gut wisdom, and our entire bodily experience are so important to include in accessing our intuitive intelligence for decision-making.

Business Application: Strategic Meetings

What applications does this have for business? An integrated approach includes using our cognitive gifts, such as being task-oriented in business, while not losing connection with the wisdom of our body. When we perform tasks and stay connected to our inner sensations, we stay in relationship with ourselves and the people around us. And at the end of the day, business is all about relationships. The more we deepen relationships, the more we build trust in our company culture and with our customer base. And people feel when we are genuine and in alignment with our care and our competence in the workplace.

How can this look in real time? Let's come back to Lisa Dion, whom we met in Chapter 3. Lisa was running a marketing meeting with her team and planning for the next calendar year in terms of strategy, webinars, and events. During the three-hour meeting, everyone was voicing their ideas, and it was getting chaotic and going in a million different directions. While everyone was inspired, Lisa started to feel overwhelmed and was losing focus.

She got more disoriented as the meeting progressed. She sensed that she wasn't the only one in the room feeling the chaotic swirl of new ideas. She felt a strong "No" swell up inside her as she knew she needed some quiet time to get centered inside herself again. She brought the room to a halt and said, "I'm feeling dysregulated and overwhelmed. That's a message for me that I need to stop, breath, and come back to my own voice inside."[19] The buzz in the room stopped immediately. Lisa's pivot forced everyone else to take a breather and also connect within themselves. This was a powerful intervention as everyone later shared that they got carried away with inspiring ideas, their own agendas, and preferences and had lost track of the common thread.

Lisa was able to feel what was happening to her body in front of the room and her tension and anxiety reduced as soon as she brought her attention within. She started to sync back up with herself and she felt a sense of calmness and clarity in returning to her body. She no longer felt lost in her head with all of the swirling thoughts. She realized that she scheduled the meeting prematurely and needed to do some more strategic thinking on her own. This strategy session was not the conversation that she needed to have with her team right now. She first needed to get clearer about her direction. Otherwise, she would let her team's inspirations and ideas pull her off course and it was too early to receive their input. She realized that she couldn't outsource some of her decisions around strategy and that it needed to come from within her first. Her team responded in kind, and they went ahead and scheduled a future meeting instead of going through the motions in this one. Lisa and the group were relieved.

Lisa used her body as a radar to detect that something felt off. She also created a company culture in which her team has the language and practice around this concept, so that she could halt a strategic meeting mid-flow and course correct as needed.

I also model and encourage team leaders and managers to listen to their gut when a conversation or a presentation is going in an unproductive direction. When you start to tune in to your body, you can actually feel when the room is going flat, when there's a chaos or anxiety of swirling ideas, or when people are shut down and hesitant to share. By learning to slow down and put our attention on what our bodies are telling us, we begin to detect the social and directional intuition of what's happening in the moment and what wants to happen next.

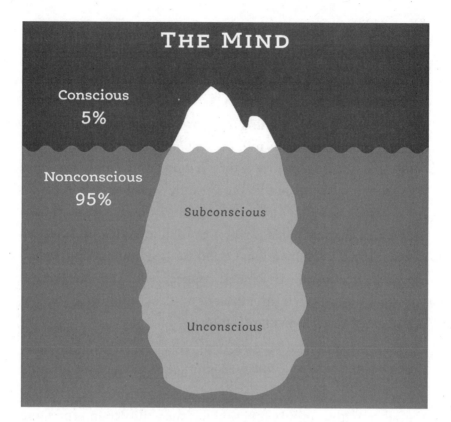

Figure 4.

The Body Is Wiser than the Mind

Through tuning into our bodies, we are accessing our deeper non-conscious, which is where intuition lives. We are able to retrieve more data to make more informed decisions, even if it's the decision to put off a decision (as in Lisa's case). By naming something when the meeting is going off track, or something is being skipped over, you are honoring your deeper intuition that your subconscious mind is picking up on. Intuition is about a relationship with the self first, and then you can have a relationship with other.

The courage to speak what you feel is what separates adaptive leadership from the status quo. In fact, neuroscience is proving that the conscious mind is running the show only 5 percent of the time, whereas the subconscious mind is shaping our experience 95 percent of the time.[20] "The joke is that that part of the mind imagines who we think we are, but it controls only 5 percent or less of our lives,"[21] says cell biologist Dr. Bruce Lipton. (See Figure 4 for a visual representation.) This is why we are short-changing ourselves if we only rely on our rational mind for decision-making. When we allow time to slow down and connect with what our body is telling us, we access our three brains and all of the information that is available in the moment.

In terms of processing speed, "the subconscious mind is more than a million times more powerful than the conscious mind."[22] According to Lipton's research, "It has been estimated that . . . the subconscious mind's function has the ability to interpret and respond to more than 40 million nerve impulses per second. In contrast, it is estimated that the diminutive self-conscious mind's prefrontal cortex can only process about 40 nerve impulses per second."[23] Yet we over value our conscious rational mind constantly. If we make time and space for our subconscious, especially in key strategic meetings and brainstorming sessions, we increase our innovative power and jump ahead of the pack.

So if listening to the body is so advantageous, why do most people avoid this? The answer lies within the fact that it means you have to feel. You have to be willing to feel the different emotions, sensations, resistance, uncertainty, blockages, belief systems, fears, and whatever may be waiting. And this may be years after learning to block out any type of hurt, pain, insecurity, uncomfortable feelings, or uncertainty. Our defenses come to the rescue and try to protect us from future hurt. Many of us learn to stay on-task and block out anything confrontational at work. However, we pay the price by hiding our vulnerability and losing the capacity to open all of our senses. As researcher and storyteller Brené Brown observed, "We cannot selectively numb emotions. When we numb the painful emotions, we also numb the positive emotions."[24] Brown reminds us that when we stay in our heads, we limit our receptivity to our environment. Not including the wisdom of our bodies limits our intuitive intelligence and is an incredible disadvantage in company engagement, communication, and decision-making.

Tom Pepple, CEO of Retail Profit Systems, started integrating his intuition with decision-making throughout the last several years after spending most of his life not being connected to this resource. "In business, and especially with the male ego, we are not taught to listen to our feelings," Tom says. "That's not how we are raised. That's not what we learn. We don't practice expressing feelings. As a male, we learn: suck it up, brush it off, and do what you think you are supposed to do or do what somebody tells you to do."[25]

Tom reached the limits of his conditioning and how this was impacting his company. For example, when something felt "off" on his cash or EBITDA reports, he wouldn't follow up with bankers in learning how this was impacting their lending decisions, even though he knew this was the right thing to do in his gut. He wasn't clear about his financial standing, which created unnecessary stress. He ignored his urge to involve employees in key decision-making that affected their routines. This eventually hurt communication and productivity. He also didn't listen when his intuition warned him about a potential partnership that resulted in the other party not keeping their contractual obligations. He spent unnecessary time and money on legal fees that proved to be stressful and costly.

Tom invested in his own leadership and personal development work outside the office and his company has been thriving since. He was able to deconstruct his old conditioning and bring a new perspective that revolutionized the business. They have more than doubled in revenue and market share, and Tom owes a lot of this to his own leadership development and learning to trust his gut. "Now when something doesn't feel right, it's a whole lot easier to recognize. It's about slowing down, not letting that adrenaline-caffeine-anxiety-gotta-get-stuff-done-today dominate my daily life."[26]

Business Application: Marketing and Technology

Marketers and advertisers have known about the power of the subconscious mind since the 1920s. Edward Bernays, the "father of spin," was the nephew of Sigmund Freud, and "was probably the first to understand the power of applying Freud's radical ideas about the human mind to business."[27] He is credited for helping lay the foundation of the marketing matrix. Bernays was heavily influenced by Freud's conclusions that "we were not always the independent, rational beings we like to think we are, but were subject to the deep, hidden urges of the subconscious mind which can influence the conscious decisions we make."[28]

Bernays put these theories into practice, and the world was never the same. One of his early clients was the Beech-Nut Packing Company of New York. He was tasked with helping them drive up sales for their main product: bacon. Bernays was challenged with changing the eating habits of Americans by moving them from the "light" Continental breakfast of juice, coffee, and bread to the "All-American Breakfast" of bacon and eggs. He knew that if he could associate bacon and eggs with health, he would influence the subconscious minds of the public.

He asked the agency's doctor for support in endorsing a hearty breakfast that included bacon. They argued the idea that because the body loses energy during sleep, it's better to have a hearty breakfast (which happened to include bacon and eggs) than a light one. He then commissioned the doctor to write to 5,000 other influential doctors and asked them leading questions in order to endorse his agenda that it's healthier to start the day with a hearty breakfast.

Shortly after Bernay's campaign, national newspapers and magazines announced that 4,500 doctors agree that a hearty breakfast is better than a lighter one.[29] Within thirty years, his marketing campaign changed the way Americans eat breakfast and what they associated as "healthy." What Sigmund Freud and Bernays knew is that our nonconscious mind is the most powerful driver and influencer in how we make decisions. The more we access our nonconscious minds through our intuition, the more empowered we can become in making our unconscious decision-making conscious.

Fast-forward to 2018. Scott Swanson, CEO of Aki Technologies in Silicon Valley, observes the same principles at play in speaking to the power of the subconscious mind. His company provides

mobile ad solutions that map the varying emotional states consumers move through in a given day, and identifies which moments present the best opportunity for their client's ad campaigns.
This is technology utilizing intuition-in-action through research,
observation, and timing. For example, by knowing when a consumer finishes a morning run intuits the most optimal moment for
Nike or Adidas to send an ad about running gear.

"That's what we are trying to do. We are trying to find those
times where we can affiliate certain products and services at the
ideal moments. The moments where the subconscious mind has
the highest propensity for having a positive association with a
product or service."[30] In other words, they are using intuition to
leverage today's technology to speak to the subconscious of their
consumers.

Intuition is used not just to target data, but to actually interpret
it for greater significance and reachability, intuiting the moment
at which the emotions and subconscious of the consumer is most
receptive. "Advertising at its best, operates on the subconscious
mind," says Swanson.[31] He points out Coca-Cola as a classic example. They sell carbonated sugar-water. Yet, for decades, they've
been associated with smiling polar bears and slogans like "Coke Is
It" to make people feel good about the brand. These associations
are super subtle and operate on the subconscious and unconscious
mind. Harnessing the power of the subconscious mind is not just
the hot topic of employees, managers, and business leaders, but
also of the customer. The subconscious is the storehouse and seat
of our deeper intelligence and its potential has been largely untapped outside of marketing.

So now that you have practiced shifting your orientation to receptivity, slowing down, quieting your inner critic, and self-doubt, you are ready to put your full attention on your body and explore what information is available to you right now. This can be done in the middle of a meeting, as shown in previous examples, or in carving out your own time when there is a big decision to be made and you need to get clear and focus. The following is an exercise that I've used with business leaders, companies, and teams to help them unlock intuitive gifts in their body and their subconscious.

Exercise: Embodied Decision-Making

Step 1: Pros and Cons

Bring to mind a decision or dilemma that you need to make on your team or in your company. It could be a new hire, letting someone go, the timing of a product launch, purchasing new equipment, creating a new product line, deciding on your yearly budget, or a number of other situations. Make a pro and con list, and use your rational mind to analyze the various points of moving forward with the decision or not. Take the time to list pros and cons, and consider the weight of each of these considerations as well. It's important to take this integrated approach and do our due diligence with the facts we know before we explore the ones we don't.

Now take a step back and review what you wrote. Take a few breaths, slow down your thinking, and see what jumps out at you when you review your list. Do you feel any sensations in your body? Do you feel any openings or closings in your heart, gut, solar plexus, or throughout your entire body? Does anything jump out at you in any direction, even if it doesn't make sense to your logical mind? Stay with this for a couple of minutes and take notes of any internal signals or cues.

Step 2: Heart Check

Close your eyes for a moment and take a few breaths to get present to your body. Let yourself relax a bit more with each breath and get out of your head and into your felt experience. What happens when you focus on your heart and you bring the dilemma up in your mind's eye? When you imagine hiring this candidate or not, or aiming your product launch for Q4, or whatever the question may be, pick one side at a time on which to focus your full attention. What happens when you bring each side of the exploration to mind? What do you notice in your heart center when you feel into these possibilities? Write down any signals you may get, which could come in the form of sensations, emotions, words, images, sounds, feelings, a sense of opening or closing, and so on. Notice strong indicators in any direction. Simply write down what you notice; don't let your rational mind sidetrack you with its commentary about what you notice.

Step 3: Gut Check

Close your eyes and bring back the same question you are presently sitting with. Take a few more breaths to resettle yourself into this moment. Remember: The present moment is the only place you can access your subconscious mind, and this is where your directional intuition lives. Your inner guidance. It may take several breaths to get out of your head brain. It can help to feel your body making contact in the chair or wherever you are sitting, so that you can stay present and in touch with your body.

Now bring your awareness into your gut. Put all of your attention there and notice what happens when you bring up the decision you are sitting with. Make time to conjure up both sides of the question you are facing. What is your gut brain telling you? Do you feel any sensations, such as warmth, cold, or tingling? Do you hear any messages or words, or get any visuals or imagery? Stay here for a moment and let yourself listen to what your gut is telling you. Open your eyes and write down your experience, no matter what your head brain thinks.

Step 4: Integration

Finally, do a full-systems check. I find it helpful to close my eyes and imagine my whole body expanding my energetic field on the inhale, and come into itself on the exhale, like the rising and falling of a wave. Practice this for a few breaths. Then, while you are present with your whole body, bring up the first part of the decision you are facing and if you should or should not move forward. Spend a few breaths listening to your body. Then move onto the other side of the decision you are facing, and repeat the same step of active listening.

What do you notice after reviewing both sides of the decision? Does one open you more? Do you feel a clear signal somewhere? Do you get a solid "No" answer about one of your decisions? Do you feel numb with one of the choices but more alive with the other? Does a sense of rightness strike you about one of the decisions, even if it's not comfortable or make sense with your mind? Write it all down.

Finally, step back and review what you've written. You've just explored the key centers from which you make conscious and subconscious decisions. Through this practice, you are integrating the best of your logic and critical thinking (Step 1), with the wisdom of your body (Steps 2 through 4).

In taking everything into consideration, what does your inner guidance tell you is the way to go? One of your options should be clearer by now because you engaged your body and mind. Now it may not be the convenient choice or the easy one, but when business leaders and managers I've worked with get clear about the right option, it's evident. I experience this as well. Once you know the right choice, you can't undo it. Ignorance *was* bliss. But the work is not over.

Conclusion

Building a relationship with the wisdom of your body is the fourth critical step in our progression. Beginning to listen to all of the signals and cues that are firing all throughout your system is the fastest track to making better decisions, as you are including a much larger data set to inform you than the rational mind alone. Yet our journey is not complete. There are a couple more key steps to put your intuition into action, which leads us to our next area of focus: asking for guidance.

Ask for Guidance

Let yourself be silently drawn by the strange pull of what you really love. It will not lead you astray.

—Rumi

Michael Lacey[1] has a history of listening to and acting on his intuition. He originally started his basement renovations company in Salt Lake City, Utah. And although it was running along nicely, he wasn't satisfied. When we started coaching together, he realized that his father had worked on basements for most of his life and that he inherited his father's dream, not his own. He felt like he was proving something to his father by trying to make the business more successful. And when his passion started to wane, he took note. He listened to his inner guidance, and knew that it was the right time to restructure Basement Renovations to something he was more passionate about: the entire home. He followed his gut and it paid off.

He rebranded and restructured his company and successfully built Highland Custom Homes, a construction company in Salt Lake City, Utah. Soon after, he joined forces with two other partners, and they grew the company from $100,000 in revenue to upward of $12 million in a few years. Their customer base and reputation were also growing rapidly and he was on the board of directors for the local homebuilder's association. They were featured in the prestigious Parade of Homes event, which showcases the best homes in the area. There were lots of indicators that showed he was successful on the outside, yet he was feeling burned out, stagnant, and not passionate about the work. This was a similar feeling to what he had before, but because this business was "his," he didn't trust it as much.

He knew something needed to change when he no longer cared about some of his customers' complaints and didn't complete the same quality of work he expected of himself. When he talked to his friends about his apathy and needing a change, they chalked it up to restlessness and convinced him to stay the course. The company was still trending upward, and Michael knew that there was no end to their growth in sight. Yet he couldn't shake the feeling that something wasn't clicking for him on the inside.

Michael recalled a couple of times in his past when he accessed his intuition and felt guided by something bigger than himself. He grew up in a spiritually oriented home that welcomed and encouraged listening to his intuition through asking for help and guidance. He felt directed by a higher wisdom in these moments and trusted this resource, yet he only remembered to make time to access this when he was in a tough spot.

In this moment, he actively prayed for guidance on how to best move forward in his life. He received no response and couldn't get a sense of his inner compass. So he'd wake up in the morning, get out of bed, put on his shoes, go to work, send the emails, put out the fires, and go back to bed. Lather, rinse, repeat. He had lost his passion, and had no sense of what needed to change.

Michael started asking himself, "What can I change in my business?" He strategized pages and pages of different ways he could improve systems or the customer experience. But even with this exercise, the hollow feeling of emptiness wouldn't leave. He sensed that his restlessness wasn't going to be solved through improving the business. There was something internally that he needed to change.

One of his partners could tell that Michael was a bit checked out and depressed, and he said, "Mike, what's going on? Why don't you take the rest of the day off?" Michael agreed and went up to the mountains above Salt Lake, looking for some guidance. While he was looking over the view of the valley, he was overcome with a strong feeling in his heart. The words came shortly afterward and he heard the message directly and clearly: "You need to quit." It was the last thing that he expected. He asked out loud, "What?" And again his inner guidance repeated, "You need to quit." This happened a few more times. He expected a role change, an extended vacation, or some lateral move in the business. Not an answer saying he needed to leave the company. He had no backup plan. He also had a family of five to care for. Yet the feeling was clear, undeniable, and felt right.

Michael was still learning to trust his guidance as it wasn't coming from his head or from the wise counsel of a mentor in his life. And this time there was even more on the line. He had a moment of doubt and fear, yet every time he asked the question, the response was unmistakable and he felt a calm underneath his thoughts that came with it. He instinctively knew that he needed to act on his intuition fast, and not give his mind a chance to backpedal. He came down from the mountain figuratively and literally, and found one of his partners at the office the next day. "I need to be bought out," Michael said.

His partner was expecting this and agreed that this felt right to him as well. All three partners then sat down and negotiated a buy-out quickly and didn't even need to go to a third-party source to get it evaluated. It was a very smooth exchange and they maintained great relationships afterward. Michael agreed to stay on an additional four months during the transition, which also bought him some time to figure out what was next.

The problem was, he had no idea what to do next. His wife was very supportive and had seen Michael successfully start up a couple of businesses. Yet there were real responsibilities they had to balance out. He had some money stowed away to invest in a new business venture, but he had to invest in any new business venture smartly.

He made some time to reflect and listen to his inner guidance. He again asked for help and listened for a response. He was in this process for two months. The tension was building as he felt the weight of providing for his family. One night, he was lying in bed and talking to his wife about random business ideas. He turned out the lights and closed his eyes. After letting his mind and body settle down, he again asked for guidance and listened to his internal system.

Bam! Just like that he sat up with his eyes wide open. He saw a flash of his next idea: It was a business that centered around his own frustrations of the delays in lending during the construction process. It was a technology platform and app that would later be called eDraw, which oversaw the money-lending process in construction. It would serve stakeholders by bringing all of the invoices to the table at once. This way, everyone involved could sign off on digital forms, and subcontractors would be notified of updates immediately, resulting in payment in ten days rather than forty-three. This would make the process easier, faster, more transparent, and less expensive. There wasn't an integrated system like this in the field that would reduce time, overhead, and increase profit between contractors, bankers, and homeowners. Banks would make more money and manage risk more effectively, general contractors would have more loyal subcontractors, subcontractors would improve their cash flow, and homeowners would get a live view into the actual finances of their home. All of them would win. He got chills as he visually downloaded the entire vision.

After asking for guidance, he knew the familiar sensations that coursed through his body and that this premonition for eDraw was coming from a deeper intelligence than his mind. He also knew that the stakes were high as he would need to leverage the house for his business and support his family with the recent buyout money. Michael later shared that, in hindsight:

I needed to make a bigger difference in the world than building houses. What I'm working on now has a potential to impact a sector of human life for good. That's what's driving me now. Looking back, there was a deeper meaning missing for me in my construction business. My growing stagnation and dissatisfaction were my intuition's way of letting me know that it was time to find my next venture. This wasn't just a career move. This was my calling. That was the felt difference and why I'm now on fire. Ninety percent of what eDraw is today was downloaded that one night.[2]

It was now clearer than ever: No matter what stage he was at in his life and whatever pressures he faced, he had to follow his intuition. This had served him countless times, even though it often tested his patience and faith. Yet he knew that his inner guidance had a plan that his mind couldn't fully comprehend. He trusted the aliveness and passion that he felt, and decided to follow this versus staying comfortable in what he knew. Michael is no different than you or I in that if we make the time and commitment to listen to our inner resources, ask the right questions, and take action from there, we will live a life on purpose and on fire.

After learning how to listen and tune into the signals and cues of your heart and gut brain as well as your whole body in the previous chapter, this one focuses on the fifth stage of deepening relationship with your intuition: asking for guidance. We'll explore how the willingness to ask a question establishes a relationship with your directional intuition, which we first talked about in Chapter 1. We'll also go over some exercises that will walk you through how to establish a relationship with your inner guidance.

Michael's story shows the vulnerability and courage that it takes to ask for guidance and wait for a response in real-life situations, which is our fifth and necessary step in listening to the deeper intelligence that is not coming from your conscious, rational mind. Recalibrating your decision-maker in this way takes time, patience, and practice, as you will need to test out the nuances of how your internal guidance system speaks to you.

Directional Intuition

Asking for guidance is the number-one way that you strengthen your directional intuition, as Michael demonstrated. He was able to tune into the wisdom of his body and ask for guidance, taking the necessary steps to find some reflective time, get away from the stress, and deal with distractions as they came up. He has built a relationship with this resource over time through testing out and trusting the process in his decision-making. The key distinction here is that his directional intuition was tuned into his higher purpose and deeper calling.

As many in business know, having a mentor, advisor, or coach in your corner that you can go to for guidance and advice is advantageous.[3] It is often one of the top ways to fast-track your growth and acceleration in whatever field you are in. Asking a mentor or advisor for guidance is critical to be a sounding board for new ideas, strategizing, and learning about your own blind spots and assumptions. Yet no one talks about developing your inner guidance and directional intuition in business so that you can refine your decision-making and discernment.

Through establishing this relationship with your inner compass, you become your own mentor and trusted advisor. This doesn't mean that you shouldn't still seek feedback outside of yourself, which is always crucial. But it does mean that you will have a better feel for how outside feedback lines up with your own tuning fork, which you have now been developing. This is a powerful way to integrate the wisdom of others and yourself.

As introduced in Chapter 1, social intuition involves emotional intelligence and a willingness to feel. The more we can get out of our heads and drop into our immediate experience, we can develop our inner radar for the nonverbal cues and signals that are happening inside of us and around us. We learn to tune into social dynamics on a deeper level and the conversation that's happening underneath the apparent conversation.

Informational intuition involves experience and pattern recognition. In time we can detect complex patterns of information for faster solutions. In Gary Klein's *The Power Of Intuition,* he reports an instance in which a seasoned NICU nurse saved a preemie's life by recognizing the beginning symptoms of sepsis that the less-experienced nurses missed.[4] If she hadn't trusted her gut sense that something about the baby "just looked funny," it probably would have been too late.[5] Beyond natural experience and pattern recognition that our subconscious mind stores, there are memorization techniques we can learn as well as speed reading and ways of accessing our subconscious mind that allow more input of data in our environment, which we'll cover in Chapter 9. We can become adept at extracting what the information is telling us and how to process and integrate it to anticipate future projections.

Directional intuition often seems the most mysterious and intangible to the outside onlooker. Directional intuition comes from listening to the wisdom of our body and subconscious, and asking for help and guidance. This one act takes us out of what we "know," and opens up the space for new input and possibilities. Asking for guidance creates an opening and receptivity for a bigger view.

We already know what we know from our rational mind perspective. Yet asking for guidance and listening to a response develops a whole new practice and channel for an internal resource of guidance and wisdom that we all have access to. And if we make the time to cultivate this relationship, we become more empowered in trusting our inherent intelligence and decision-making abilities. And as Michael demonstrates, our inner decision-maker leads us toward a life of passion, purpose, and fulfillment when we are living from this resource.

Scott Swanson, the CEO of Aki Technologies, who we met in Chapter 6, relies on his directional intuition as a business leader. He has had some profound experiences in asking for guidance at certain decision points in his career that helped him build trust in this resource over time. Previous to cofounding Aki Technologies, Scott had tech job at which he was beginning to feel unhappy. He wanted to get some clarity on whether he should stick it out or not. One day, he had the impulse to have a conversation with his body, something he had rarely done before. He asked his body to show him a sign if he was to continue at this position. At one point, he even said out loud, "Well, if I'm really unhappy, my body will tell me."[6]

Then he remembered the exact moment. He was doing laundry about a week later after he made this proclamation. And out of nowhere, red spots broke out over his entire body. He had never experienced anything like that before and he didn't know what it was, so he visited the doctors and they also didn't know what it was. The doctors wanted him to stay out of the office as a result. Even though he had a doctor's note to stay home in order to prevent others from becoming infected, his employer really didn't like the fact that he was staying at home and this exposed the tension between them.

Soon after this issue, they began the process of separating. The impetus came from feeling something "off" in the company culture and asking for guidance. His body sent a message that he shouldn't be at this office and to stay at home. Scott thinks that the spots were not just stress-induced, but also a physical manifestation of his unhappiness. He mentioned that he didn't know what made him think about asking his body for feedback, but he did, and it responded. He has since used his body as a tuning fork for key decisions in his business, such as hiring, acquiring other businesses, and product development. Asking for guidance has given him results that he wouldn't have come to otherwise. He reports that in asking the question and staying open to a response, his attention eventually gets laser-focused on a specific direction as other options naturally start to fall away. His intuition remains clear and steady when he allows proper time to listen.

Asking for guidance naturally puts us in a receptive space of not knowing, of being truly open, and cultivating patience and deep listening. These qualities serve us in other areas of life in being more effective communicators. The major upside here is that we all need help and support in moving beyond our current challenges and sticking points. Asking for guidance invites a deeper conversation from within that is the hallmark of building our intuitive intelligence—the most intimate resource available to us.

The Four Components of Asking for Guidance

There are four components of asking for guidance that will help you develop a deeper relationship with your directional intuition and inner compass.

1. Ask Powerful Questions

To receive the right guidance, you need to ask the right questions. How you frame a question can make all the difference. By taking time out, letting your mind slow down, and tuning into your body, you are now in the perfect space to ask for guidance on any question that has your attention. Most business owners that I coach get in trouble when they no longer make time for strategic thinking, which is where they take time to inquire and reflect on the company's direction or on their approach.

To ask the right questions means that you have to suspend certainty. In Bernadette Jiwa's book *Hunch,* she reminds us that "every breakthrough idea starts not with a surefire solution, but with a difficult or puzzling question. Innovation, creativity, and invention happen in the uncertain pursuit of truth and with a desire to solve a problem."[7] The greatest inventions and innovations have happened from those who ask powerful questions and listen to the responses from their emotions and intuition.

I had the pleasure of spending a week in west Ireland with poet and business consultant David Whyte, who is a master at asking powerful questions. He shared with us a powerful question for when you are facing a dilemma in your business or your life. In this situation, you can ask yourself, "Do you want the future of the person who goes this way or that?" This question immediately puts you into a larger mindset on tackling the issue at hand. And then you can use your skill of listening to how your body and being respond. A similar question tailored to your business would be "Do you want the future of the company that goes this way or that?" Imagine the fork in the road that you are facing, or whatever decision point you are up against. Then ask this question when you are in a reflective space. Let the silence do the work after you ask your question, and engage in deep listening to discover the response within.

2. Lean Into Vulnerability

Asking for guidance makes us vulnerable. We have to be willing to not know. And in the business world, this goes against the idea that we always need to look like we have the answers, and where uncertainty is looked down upon. As Jiwa writes, "We are in danger of becoming a generation of plugged-in, look-it-uppers who are more ready to take things at face value and less willing to inquire or explore. More satisfied with proof and less open to discovery . . . more fearful of uncertainty than open to possibility."[8] When we can admit that we don't know the answers, we lean into the uncertainty, which is the doorway to possibility.

A couple qualities that you see in staff who lead include a willingness to ask for help and having the ability to receive input. They are the ones who are hungry to learn and don't hold themselves back in getting the answers and feedback they are seeking. Showing that we don't know something and that we are curious to learn is a strength and shows resourcefulness. Brené Brown has made a career out of researching vulnerability and shame. She says, "Vulnerability sounds like truth and feels like courage. Truth and courage aren't always comfortable, but they're never weakness."[9] Understanding the role of vulnerability and not knowing is one of the fundamentals to unlocking the potential of our intuitive intelligence.

Asking for guidance involves an act of surrender. We are surrendering our certainty and the world that we know to new possibilities. We are choosing to leave the confines of the comfort zone of our best thinking and analysis. We are opening up the space to a bigger view and a larger conversation. And this can only happen if we choose to suspend or surrender our assumptions and beliefs. Critical thinking and analysis are crucial in decision-making, yet when you are stuck on the same problem over and over, it's time for a fresh approach. Leaning into the vulnerability of not knowing is a prerequisite for connecting with your intuitive intelligence.

3. Invest in the Process, Let Go of the Outcome

If we want to cultivate an honest and active relationship with our inner guidance, we need to stay open to asking a question for that guidance and not being attached to the outcome or response. If we try to control the response with our personal preferences and biases, or what is comfortable, we sabotage accessing our intuition. Our personal agendas get in the way and distort our inner knowing. Being able to receive these messages clearly requires that we stay receptive and open to what our body and subconscious are telling us. We have to practice letting go of control of our preferred outcomes in order to truly surrender to our deeper intelligence.

We might get a response that doesn't fit our "picture" and doesn't seem practical, convenient, comfortable, or even something that we want. Intuition works on a different frequency, and often there are messages and a direction waiting for us that don't yet make sense to the conscious, rational mind. As mentioned previously, intuition is not linear and might anticipate scenarios that your mind can't yet grasp. Your intuitive voice will often lead you toward what you and your business *need*, not simply what you want.

4. Patience

Staying in the question for as long as it takes is one of the most difficult aspects of building a relationship with your intuition. This requires great patience. Intuition doesn't operate on your time scale. Are you willing to stay with the question that you are asking, even if you don't get a response right away? This can be especially challenging when you are in a place of pressure or stress. Yet any question worth asking is worth getting an answer to. The more you are willing to give proper time and attention on a sincere decision that you are facing, the more you are building trust with your inner navigational system as an instrument to serve you. This is how you learn that you can trust what you feel, and that there are profound wisdoms that you carry inside of you. And the more you practice this, the more you will strengthen this tool and relationship.

Over time, you begin to learn the language of your inner guidance and develop a trustable connection with your own discernment. You may know people around you who have a really deep connection with their intuition, whether it's in certain areas of their business, in life, or all around. This is something that we can all build through practice. Asking for guidance and listening to the response is where the dialogue of inner empowerment begins.

Exercise: Red Light, Green Light

I adapted the following exercise used by Lisa Dion, the founder of Synergetic Play Therapy whom we met in Chapter 3, and I've found it very effective. It has to do with call and response, the core components of conversation and relationship. When you have a big decision to make in your business or in your life, try this Red Light, Green Light exercise to get clearer on what your inner compass is directing you toward. "Red light" simply refers to a no, or some type of pause or holding pattern from moving forward in the decision you are facing. A "green light" is a clear yes. You can apply the following exercise to key business situations, life transitions, and any major or minor decision that you are sitting with.

Clear the Space

Get into a mindful state that has you feeling calm and where you won't be distracted. Turn off your electronics, find a comfortable posture, and allow yourself to come back to your body and your breath. If you are in a strong emotional state, as in feeling very anxious, stressed, or depressed, you may need to spend more time feeling through those feelings until they subside a bit. This way, you can be in a clearer space that is not as colored by strong emotions, which will allow more ability to listen to the voice of your intuition.

Say It Out Loud

Bring the decision to mind that you are considering. Say whatever it is out loud. So you might say "launch this product," or "sign this contract," or "open up a new location," or "hire this person." Now after you say the decision out loud that you are sitting with, watch what happens in your body. If you get no response, keep steady in this state and repeat the question every so often. It's important to allow the silence in between to pull the answers out of you. The more you can get quiet and listen, the more likely you will get a response from your subconscious. Keep working to quiet your rational mind and let yourself slow down and breathe in the silence. The more still you become, the more you will notice your body talking to you.

Decode Your Intuitive Language

As you practice this continually, you will learn what the red lights and green lights feel like in your body. Watch for anything that goes into a "holding back" posture. If there's any tension or tightening up, then it very well may be a red light, which means it's a no, or that it's not time yet to move forward in the decision. If there's a green light, perhaps you feel an opening, or a warm sensation throughout your body, or a sense of relaxedness and peace. You'll have to learn how your cues and signals speak to you over time.

For me, I don't often get a strong "no" sensation unless it's an urgent matter. I usually get a hollow or empty feeling in my solar plexus when it's a "no" or not time to move forward. My green light usually consists of a warmth or fullness in my solar plexus area. This has become a trustable indicator for me and has made it easier to locate my own intuitive radar. I try to pay attention to my full bodily experience for any signs and cues, but my solar plexus seems to be the center of my own yes or no. The key is to find out over time what your red light and green light look and feel like in your experience. Once again you may get words, images, sounds, sensations, feelings, and so on. Once you learn your intuitive language, you can say to yourself, "Please speak to me. Give me a sign that I can detect. Help make it clear if I should choose this way or that." And then let silence do the work. Witness how your body responds based on your inner signals and cues. Stay curious and open; the more that you practice, the more you will cultivate your inner decision-maker.

Follow the Rabbit Hole

If you get a red-light response, it's worth going one step further and question if it is truly a "no" or just a fear. Remember: It's easy for your inner critic and comfort zones to hijack the process. It's really important to start to distinguish for yourself what your intuitive "no" feels like versus the voice of your inner critic (as we covered in Chapter 5).

You can ask follow up questions such as, "Is it fear that's holding me back?" or "Is it a true 'no'?" or "Is it just a timing issue?" Then you can continue the same practice of asking and listening to get more detail on the situation. Once again, a question worth asking is worth getting a response. This can be really challenging when the response is not comfortable or convenient. If there is fear or doubt, you will often hear a lot of back and forth or convincing yourself of a certain direction, versus a clear response. Or you might get a real "no," and then the critic will come in and try to convince you otherwise. Follow this through until you feel clear with what your inner guidance is stating. These are the moments during which you are opening to a higher intelligence that your conscious, rational mind doesn't have access to. And the business men and women I know who are putting this into practice are on the leading edge of their purpose, creativity, and fulfillment.

Exercise: The Coin Toss

Another way that you can test your directional intuition is to think about a decision that you are considering and to flip a coin ten times. Now assign one part of the decision—hiring a new manager in Q3—to heads, and the other side of the decision—postponing until a future quarter—to tails. When you flip the coin ten times, simply notice which side you are rooting for internally. You will most likely feel an excitement or draw to one of these sides. You'll rarely feel completely neutral when you listen to the nuances in your body.

Your subconscious is speaking to you as you are flipping the coin again and again. You'll notice a leaning toward wanting it to be heads or tails. It's not about how many times it lands on heads or tails, which comes from the rational mind perspective of percentages and numbers. Instead, it's about using this process to recognize the internal signals and cues that your bodily intelligence is leading you toward. See what happens when you listen! In hindsight you will really learn if this particular exercise serves you or not. You can start with more minor decisions and then build up to larger ones when you get more confidence.

Conclusion

Asking for guidance is the fifth step in deepening your relationship with your intuitive intelligence. This process builds trust as you get to learn about how your decision-maker operates. With practice, you build this reputation with yourself and discover all of the nuances of your intuitive signs, cues, and languaging. This resource can now be integrated with the different sets of data or other people's perspectives and opinions, and gives you a stronger place to make decisions from, as you are more connected to your conviction on what is right for you. Once we can identify and hear what our intuition is saying, we come to the final step: acting on it.

ACT ON YOUR INNER INTELLIGENCE

Creativity requires something more than the processing of information. It requires human thought, spontaneous intuition and a lot of courage.

—Akio Moriata, cofounder of Sony

Darcy Winslow[1] picked up the phone and fielded the customer's question: "Hi, where can I find the Goddess product?" Darcy was puzzled and replied, "We don't have a Goddess product. Nike Goddess stores are where you can find women's Nike apparel and footwear." Afterward, Darcy hung up the phone and was struck by the exchange. Then everything came to a standstill. She felt a flash of energy run through her body. It had never occurred to her before, but in that moment, a big insight hit her: "Why don't we create a Goddess collection that is designed specifically for women, and run our women's business differently than men, based on how women shop and work out?" Within seconds, she felt completely inspired and saw a vision of what she needed to do to spearhead this insight into action. At the same time, she knew it wouldn't be easy to implement because of the male-dominated culture within the Nike corporation at the time.

As soon as she got off the phone, she walked over to Angela Snow, one of Nike's top creative directors, and shared her insight about designing a women's collection that would change the company's mindset in how they approached and made products for women. Angela's eyes opened wide. She sensed the intuitive impulse that they were onto something; they could both feel it. Soon they were off to the races in strategizing and designing what this could look like.

At the time, Darcy was the general manager of women's performance footwear at Nike, but she originally started out as a biomechanical researcher in their sports research lab. "I remember the guy who originally hired me in the lab. Within a month, he said, 'I'm going to fast-track you. I just have a gut sense that you have got some things to do at Nike.'"[2] Being recognized by her boss gave her even more confidence to trust her gut in business decisions and confirmed that she was on the right track.

She integrated her intuitive decision-making to stay a step ahead, and quickly rose up the ranks through product creation and running the Global Research Design and Development division, which included advanced R&D. In the mid-1990s, when climate change was barely on the radar, she led the integration of sustainability into the heart of the business, such as moving away from greenhouse gases that were found in their air soles. She was committed to steering Nike toward being a leader for good and used her intuition to anticipate where the market was moving.

It was at this time that another one of her bosses recognized her intuitive leadership and visionary qualities, and asked her to create the women's footwear division and run it. She said yes, even though she had some apprehension. In the past, there were at least three different attempts to create a woman-specific business that failed for different reasons. Almost all of their studies in the research lab were done on men, but women are not small men and girls are not small boys.

They were operating from an idea they called "shrink it and pink it." The idea was to take a man's product, shrink it down, change the color to pink, and sell it. Darcy intuitively felt that this was the wrong approach. Instead, they needed to make the best possible product for women athletes through investing in proper research. Darcy's team started analyzing the physiological and biomechanical differences of women's feet and how they scale. For any given shoe size, a woman weighs 15 to 40 percent less than a man. So offering the same stiffness or cushioning in the shoe didn't make sense. These new innovative questions were never taken seriously enough in the past.

Darcy and her team eventually created a product collection based on their research, which would officially be called Sport Lux, to test out her hunch. In other words, she was innovating a collection in order to help change a mindset. Her inspired vision was not just about a change in biomechanics, but a change in Nike's approach to how women shop. One of the key differences they found was that men most often identify with the sport they played as a kid growing up. "I played football" or "I was a runner." Women take a multi dimensional approach to their fitness activity: "I work out in the gym, I take aerobic classes, I do yoga, and I sometimes run." They saw themselves as multi dimensional in the sports realm, yet women's product lines were not reflecting this.

Darcy was amazed when she reflected on how quickly that one customer call sparked something inside of her and changed the trajectory of her own destiny and that of Nike. Yet there were some internal grumblings within the company, as some senior management still didn't see the point of women having a separate division. In fact, the board even objected to the name "Nike Goddess" stores, and they were eventually changed to "Nike Women's." The irony here is that Nike is the Greek goddess of victory. Darcy had to dig deep to stay connected to her intuition and stay the course on shifting how people thought about women in sports inside the company and beyond. Her intuition was tested, but she knew that she needed to champion her gut sense.

Part of the intuition was, and this was true in the sustainability work when nobody cared about that nor knew what it was, was knowing that there was a better way of being in the world of what Nike could be. If I approached this work with the best of intentions, it almost didn't matter what the outcome was. And I just had to follow that thread, stay connected to my inner guidance, and keep taking action on what needed to happen next.[3]

After all of the research, design, and preparation, it was time to launch Sport Lux. This collection was a combination of high performance and bling that was created and marketed just for women. It was all set to be introduced on Valentine's Day and was only going out to their Nike Goddess stores. It had taken one and a half years to get every facet of the pipeline to execute this one-day delivery successfully and quietly. In Darcy's own words, "We didn't talk about the launch in product reviews, we didn't go through the entire public release, so we kept it as under the radar so it wouldn't get cut before we even had a chance to test out our theory."[4] She had gone through her checklists multiple times and finally had to relax. There was nothing else to do.

That next day, the entire collection arrived at Nike Goddess stores across the country and completely sold out. The response was loud and clear: It was a success. The Sport Lux collection gave Nike the confidence that they could speak to women differently and that they could create a completely different aesthetic that also performed. The women's footwear division was here to stay, and men had to listen. Testing her inner sense and taking action on her intuition paid off. She later headed Nike's Global Women's Footwear, Apparel and Equipment business, and continued to innovate better products and approaches for women.

After leaving Nike, Darcy continues to trailblaze across sectors and make an impact as she integrates intuition and action. She now serves as president of The Academy for Systems Change, which she cofounded with Peter Senge and others. Here she continues to help teach other individuals, teams, and organizations how to listen to and take action on their intuitive guidance in systems change solutions across multiple arenas.[5]

Taking action is the sixth and final step in building a relationship with your intuition as you bring that spark of knowing and insight into existence. You carve out new pathways that didn't exist before. If you are not the guardian and steward of your inner wisdom, who will be? We don't honor ourselves if we don't act on what we feel. And by "feel," I don't mean reactivity that's coming from fear or insecurity. I mean responding from the feeling and sensing that comes from our intuitive intelligence. Our deeper knowing. If we don't listen to this intimate relationship with ourselves that we've been cultivating, this resource will fade away into the background. Just like how a muscle atrophies if we don't use it, the same happens with our intuition. This happens over time if we outsource our inner knowing to our doubts, fears, and the strong opinions of others around us.

We often choose to override our inner intelligence because following it isn't convenient, doesn't always feel good, or appears risky and brings up fear of venturing outside our comfort zone. But life isn't about taking action only when the action is comfortable. It's about trusting a deeper wisdom that comes from listening to what wants to happen. And often our intuition will guide us to make decisions that are beyond our personal preferences for the greater good, which we might not comprehend through our rational minds in the moment. In hindsight, we often see that following our inner sense was exactly what led to creating a greater impact than we could have generated from our best thinking. By acting on our inner intelligence, we honor ourselves and stand for our highest values. We become allies with ourselves on a profound level, as our actions are in alignment with our convictions. We lead in business when we're congruent from our innermost core to our outermost actions. And taking action on our intuition keeps us on our leading edge of growth. So let's take a look at four components of taking action on your inner guidance.

1. Insight Alone Is Not Enough

How many times have you known the right path to take, yet hesitated in taking action? Perhaps you knew when you were accommodating a customer that wasn't the right fit, or that your team was reaching its capacity to deliver to your clients and that you needed to bring on more staff, but didn't do anything about it? Perhaps you've seen a company hesitate from investing in more training for staff and it's clearly hurting the business, yet no one is speaking up? Many people stay in dead-end jobs and relationships even though they know they need to leave. In other words, insight alone is not enough. There's often a gap between seeing what needs to happen and acting on it. If you aren't living your most fulfilling, purposeful life, your intuition will remind you, and sometimes haunt you, that you know what you need to do.

Insight is mental and often accompanies an intuitive feeling or sense. It's the "aha moment" that people refer to. And although awareness is a necessary step in taking a new direction, we need to mobilize and put our insight into practice. This is where a lot of business leaders and managers have a gap, which I see in coaching all the time. They know what they need to do and what feels right, yet there might be unconscious emotional blocks that get in the way from following through.

Analysis paralysis is a common roadblock in decision-making, as the decision gets postponed due to some version of fear of moving forward or making the wrong choice. In the famous "Jam Study," psychologists Sheena Iyengar and Mark Lepper found that consumers were ten times more likely to purchase jam on display when the number of jams available was reduced from twenty-four to six.[6] Less choice equals more sales in some circumstances. This is why a restaurant menu that seems to offer everything can seem less appetizing than a simplified version.

I've seen this type of hesitation cost businesses millions of dollars and unnecessary stress and anxiety because they did not put their insights into action. Take a coaching client of mine, Emilio from Atlanta, who was painfully turning away business as his team was at maximum capacity in building websites. The soonest that they could deliver a website to a new client was nine months out. They lost two million dollars from the previous year due to lost website sales and ancillary services. Emilio knew that he needed to track billable hours more closely to make sure that his team was focusing on the right tasks, as well as hiring an additional web development team to tackle the workload.

The analysis paralysis of spending more money stopped him in his track for six months as he paused on making a decision, even though the data was clear that something needed to change. Business continued to decline as clients didn't want to wait that long for a new website. Eventually he followed his intuition and acted on his insight that spending money on incoming staff and productivity training was the risk he needed to take to grow. It eventually paid off. His team was able to streamline their processes and had the manpower to reduce the wait time down to three months. They also redesigned their packaged services with a focus on recurring revenue and profits soared. Taking action on the insights that were sparked from his intuition is what finally made the difference.

If you let your doubts and fears sabotage your progress, you won't blaze new trails that your inner guidance is leading you toward. It might take personal development work and practice to overcome these doubts and fears so that you can build up the confidence and muscle memory to act on what you know needs to happen next. One of the keys to moving your awareness from insight to action is to stay connected to your purpose or the bigger picture that you are working toward. When you are crystal clear about what motivates you, you can use this as a catalyst to break down simple action steps that you can work on each day and each week, which move you steadily toward your vision. Aligning your daily action steps with your larger goals and objectives will give you the fuel to bring your insights into reality.

2. Courage

Growth happens on the border of challenge and support. Listening to, trusting, and acting on your intuition takes courage because you are being asked to leave familiar territory for uncertain shores with no guarantee of reward. Yet this act alone differentiates you as a leader in business and beyond because most of the world is not operating from this place of living on the edge of growth. Courage comes from the Latin word *cor* and the old French word *curage,* both meaning "heart." Courage is taking action from the heart, no matter the adversity you are facing. It's about standing in the face of fear and uncertainty and still moving forward. Courage is often the necessary ingredient to take your insights into action, as mentioned previously. And with today's inundation of information, analytics, and spreadsheets, it can feel risky to go against these metrics in terms of decision-making and tuning into your deeper intelligence within. In fact, the greater the adversity and doubters you may be up against, the greater the courage it takes to listen to and act on your values and convictions.

Jayson Gaddis[7] was a therapist with a full practice, six-figure income, and a wait list. He had reached the pinnacle of his career and achieved what most therapists dream about when they leave graduate school and hang out their shingle for business. He enjoyed it for a little while, but then he felt restless inside and knew that there was something more for him. He wasn't satisfied with what he had achieved and was getting the message that there was a bigger calling beyond the confines of a therapist's office. Everyone around him had ideas of what he should do, and many suggested staying the course. Yet he couldn't ignore the deeper feeling inside. He was being guided toward his next stage of growth, even though he didn't know what that was.

Without a safety net, he closed his practice and made space for what was next. He had cut the cord before and trusted in his gut sense about what he needed to do. He just didn't know what the next evolution would look like. This time, the stakes were higher because he had two kids. He had to wade through massive amounts of fear and anxiety around money, but he still moved forward knowing that this was the right step in his career path. He set out to create a new business and did a crash course in marketing. He wanted to get his teachings out to a wider audience. He took the necessary action steps to fulfill his inner calling that wouldn't go away.

Jayson let his inner compass guide him, which led him to creating the Smart Couple Podcast and the Relationship School, which teaches people "the class that they never got in school": having healthy and vibrant intimate relationships. He is able to reach more people than he ever could have as a therapist while providing comfortably for his family. He knew that he needed to dig deep into the courageous path of trusting himself and venturing into new territory. When describing what it feels like to follow his directional intuition, Jayson says, "It's a mix of fear and this gnawing feeling that I cannot let go of. It eats at me every day until I listen to it. When I listen to it and go toward that feeling, new doors and possibilities emerge that scare me and excite me. Logic enters, but the feeling is stronger. And then I just follow that 'felt sense.' When I truly honor that feeling, it guides me to the next chapter, the next big challenge that I'm here to meet."[8]

The more you practice building a relationship with your intuition and integrating it into everyday life, the more you will experience this resource as a gift that's there to serve your larger mission or calling. And everyone benefits when you are living a life on-purpose as this passion and aliveness become contagious. Life will test your convictions. If you take a stand based on what you feel, you will be questioned by other colleagues and authorities around you who may not have the same sense, or they may be jealous because they are not coming from a similar place of empowerment. In those moments, the key is to be able to stay open to other perspectives and taking them into account, without letting this divert you from your true north. This is where dialogue and brainstorming can create new possibilities that neither you nor the other party realized in the first place. This happens when both sides stay curious in the conversation and are willing to hear each person's position for what's in the best interest of everyone.

I have found that it's easier to build momentum by first practicing with smaller decisions that don't have potentially severe consequences. The more you practice taking action on what you intuitively feel in these moments, you will build greater confidence for the larger decisions that you are facing. You will once again earn this reputation with yourself and feel much more certainty in facing the doubters or naysayers around you as well as the critic inside.

Interestingly enough, when you are truly congruent with your values, convictions, and intuitive knowing, people around you will feel this too. While it takes courage to follow through on action steps as Jayson demonstrated, especially when it goes against the norms of the group or marketplace, it will become easier over time, and the payoff is living a more fulfilling and meaningful life.

3. Commitment

Another key component of acting on your intuition is centered on committing to this practice as a way of life. Whereas courage helps you bring insight into action, it takes a commitment of consistent effort over time for transformation to happen. We all get into habitual patterns that make it difficult to change behavior. And if we don't try new approaches, we won't have new outcomes. By being receptive and creating space to listen to what new information your subconscious mind is picking up on, you have an opportunity to innovate only if you are committed to following through and putting these hunches into action.

Micha Mikailian[9] is a self-described serial entrepreneur. He started his first company when he was a teenager and has now launched eight businesses over the span of twenty years. From owning a real estate company to his recent tech venture called Intently, which is a platform that replaces Internet ads with personalized affirmations to help users show up as their highest self in life, he attributes intuition as a differentiating leadership skill to cultivate. "I made a commitment that I would follow my intuition 100 percent of the time, no matter what it tells me," says Micha. "And that commitment for me was my 'aha moment' and my turning point because that opened up a whole new world of what is possible with intuition if you just fully surrender into it."[10]

Micha shares that there are times when he's required to listen to his intuition multiple times before he realizes the bigger-picture message that's taking place. For example, he had just hired a creative team to build a launch video for his company. And although he was working with them in the conference room, he knew at that moment that this was not the right team and this was not the right time. He had just went through a lengthy selection process and built a contract with them. Yet he stopped the meeting. He let them know that he was committed to following his intuition 100 percent of the time and that he was not feeling inspired to work on this launch. They ended up canceling the project, and although he lost some of the money he put down, he trusted this step.

A few months later, he was invited to Richard Branson's Necker Island with a group of entrepreneurs and was asked to stay for another week. There were some really interesting people coming to the island, and he was willing to reschedule anything to make that happen. How could he say no to that? As soon as he accepted, his intuition told him he had to go home instead. The message was clear and undeniable. He had practiced building this resource for years and knew not to ignore this voice. His mettle was tested as he was getting so many entrepreneurial revelations from being there. Yet he honored his commitment and made the twenty-four-hour journey home with multiple boat and plane rides.

He was on the last leg of his journey, catching up on emails, and he received a Facebook notification that there was a party at his friend's house that night. He told himself, "There's no way I am going out to a party tonight." Yet his intuition said, "No, you have to go to this party." He looked at the timing and by the time his plane landed, he would only be there for the last twenty to thirty minutes. He tried to talk himself out of it, and his inner guidance system wasn't having it. So he went to the party. Once he arrived with all of his luggage, he sat on the couch and heard this artist playing a set of music. He introduced the next song and said that the inspiration for it came when he was sitting in a yoga studio and saw all of these beautiful affirmations on the wall.

As soon as Micha heard it, he knew that this was the theme song for their new launch, and he saw the whole video appear before his eyes. It was almost as if the song was created for his business. In fact, after he approached the artist at the end of the song, the artist said, "I'm so glad you found me. I had the intuition that this song was meant for somebody who's creating a platform." He asked, "Are you building a platform to bring more intention into people's lives?" Micha said, "Yes, it's called Intently."[11] It turns out that the artist created the song within a week of when Micha said no to the people in the conference room several months prior.

As Micha's story demonstrates, you might not see the bigger picture in the moment. Your intuitive messaging might not make sense given the current circumstances. Yet you will see the greater wisdom that your directional intuition is guiding you toward with practice and experience. And it often takes putting this into action to really test out this inner resource and your commitment to using it.

Are you willing to test this out for six months? Find out for yourself what can change when you fully dedicate your attention to building a relationship with your inner navigational system and learn to trust and act on it no matter what your mind or other people's perceptions tell you. With this level of commitment, you will forge a new relationship with your inner guidance and see how this plays out in everyday ways and for larger decisions as well.

4. Adaptive Leadership

The fourth component of acting on your inner guidance results in what is called "adaptive leadership." Adaptive leadership is the ability to embrace new skills and approaches that are in response to a changing environment. It is all about taking in the relevant data around you and adapting accordingly. Utilizing intuitive decision-making immediately puts you in a receptive orientation that allows you to be more adaptive and resilient, as you are listening to your surroundings in a deeper way, and then engaging in real-time action. Adaptive leadership is highlighted by your ability to respond, not react.

Cate Stephenson,[12] who cofounded Surfsong Resort on Tortola, British Virgin Islands, attests to the power of listening as a key function of her intuition, which has allowed her to adapt to change. Cate shares that "intuition is my first responder and the first thing that I listen to as a leader. I make the choice to listen first, so that I am not reactive. Too many times people's responses can be too quick. If you are already listening to your intuition, you're listening from a deeper place."[13] By following your intuition, you are actually calming down your decision-making process, and you are letting your company be more balanced and sustainable as a result. There is now more space for well-rounded input, and better decision-making is possible.

From the volatile economy to climate change, our ability to be adaptive leaders is a critical skill to harness. Part of being adaptive, according to Darcy Winslow, is to be willing to put your own egoic needs aside in service of the larger ecosystem and the greater good. When Darcy and her team work with organizations, she asks the question:

> *How do they look twenty years out and start to adapt their business model accordingly? In their investments, innovation, in research and technology, whatever it might be. If companies can develop their intuitiveness, and if companies can be courageous, companies can be adaptive. Yet this only works if the leaders themselves are adaptive.*[14]

Darcy reminds us that we are all leaders in this way when we are willing to listen to our deeper intelligence and take courageous action from this place. It's no secret that a company culture takes on the values and characteristics of its leadership team. Our organizations and/or departments will always be a reflection of us and our level of self-awareness, growth, and willingness to adapt to change. The more we can include our intuitive intelligence in the decision-making process, the more likely our company will be more agile in anticipating and responding to adversity.

Conclusion

When we complete this sixth step of acting on what we feel, we give ourselves a chance to live a more fulfilling life. When our actions are aligned with our deepest calling, we thrive. It takes putting the four components of our insights into action, which takes courage, as we stand for what we believe in. And when we commit to acting on our inner guidance, we become more adaptive and resilient to the ever-changing environment around us. Business leaders and managers who adopt this principle have a clear advantage over those who are stuck in spreadsheets and the opinions of others alone, and are—by definition—not leading. When you are connected to this innermost resource, you are naturally more in resonance with the flow of life and not getting in the way of a deeper intelligence. Action is what brings your intuitive impulses into reality where you can make change happen.

MAKE YOUR COMPANY CULTURE SMARTER

I skate to where the puck is going to be, not where it has been.

—Wayne Gretzky

Intuitive intelligence is the missing link in helping your company culture stay ahead of today's challenges and better anticipate the ones to come. It's revolutionary because most of us have been conditioned out of our innate intelligence as we over-rely on metrics and outside opinions. By doing the work to reconnect with this incredible resource, we have access to more data and can make more well-informed decisions, as we include all of ourselves in the decision-making process.

We have spent a good amount of attention on how to access and develop intuitive skills, as well as the benefits of cultivating intuitive intelligence in your company and on your teams. Now let's focus on how to create the right conditions in your business environment for intuitive decision-making to catalyze effective communication, creativity, and innovation. We'll also explore how to implement directional, social, and informational intuition in practical ways that help your company and teams stay ahead, as well as how to assess and advance intuitive intelligence within your organization.

Leaders Go First

Leaders set the tone for their company culture. In order for intuitive decision-making to integrate into your strategy and activities, it has to start with members of the leadership team respecting and honoring their own intuition first. If leaders don't understand or learn how to decode their own internal signals, they will miss these cues in their environment. This is a skill that needs to be developed over time. It's a journey. Yet there are more resources than ever to learn the language of your own inner guidance system. You can start by simply asking, "What's my own internal feedback system telling me?" In hindsight, were there any signals that were speaking to you during the decision-making process? It's important to start noting and tracking the specific ways that you receive information. This is your superpower.

It is risky for anyone in a company to share a gut sense about business decisions that might be unpopular or seem out of nowhere. Leaders put themselves at even greater risk as every decision they make is more scrutinized. Yet for leaders to truly lead, they are required to lean into their own discomfort and be willing to make decisions that might not be well received or might fail. As Patrick Lencioni reminds us:

The only way for the leader of a team to create a safe environ-ment for his team members to be vulnerable is by stepping up and doing something that feels unsafe and uncomfortable first. By getting naked before anyone else, by taking the risk of making himself vulnerable with no guarantee that the other members of the team will respond in kind, a leader demon-strates an extraordinary level of selflessness and dedication to the team. And that gives him the right, and the confidence, to ask others to do the same.[1]

The more a leader is willing to break the ice and model the behavior he or she expects to see, the more likely these values will be reflected in the company culture and others will learn that it's okay to take risks, which is necessary for innovation to take place.

Leaders can foster intuitive decision-making if they develop qualities such as receptivity, openness, vulnerability, curiosity, play, emotional intelligence, a willingness to not know, and mak-ing time to listen to their inner and outer environment. If they are not a living example of what they want to see on their teams, no one will take them seriously. As Lisa Dion notes,

The culture and the climate of a business changes when the leader leads from their intuition and encourages that from their employees. It can be scary territory. But when they do, there's a deeper connection with their staff, because you are not leading from this left-brain, "get it done" place. Your heart's in it. You can see people more clearly. There's a larger appreciation for your team and the journey you are on.[2]

This is a great time to reflect: Are you carving out time for reflective and strategic thinking? Are you facilitating meetings and solo time for outside-the-box thinking and encouraging others to do the same? When people come to you for answers, do you respond with questions that help others dig deeper into their own intuitive solutions? And most importantly, what are you doing to grow these skill sets in order to foster a transformative and innovative company culture?

Safety and Trust: The Bedrock of Intuition

There's an interesting paradox between risk and safety. In order for a culture or a group of people to take a risk, they have to feel safe. So if you want to encourage risk-taking and thinking strategically and creatively outside the box, and even being willing to look like a fool at the meeting for a moonshot idea, there has to be a culture of safety and acceptance for an employee to relax into themselves and share their gifts. In fact, Google conducted a two-year study and found that the highest-performing teams had one thing in common: psychological safety.[3]

According to Jim Oakley, a former member of the global staffing management team at Google for twelve years, creating a culture of trust is one of the main reasons that Google has thrived. They've cultivated a sense of respect and safety for employees to share openly in company meetings. He observes: "The best companies like Google reward managers who are going to listen to their staff and really solicit feedback. And they will do it in settings where the leaders can be present and accountable to what is being communicated."[4] He also adds that the best managers "know how to pick up nonverbal communication like body language, tone of voice, and to listen for whether or not there is agreement in the room."[5] How Google navigates recent allegations that some employees don't feel as safe to speak their mind as they used to[6] will dictate company success.

An atmosphere of open communication, respect, and creativity is infectious and directly serves the company because employee participation is encouraged. As Jim observes, "Ambitious ideas communicate that you are part of a company and something larger that takes risks. The 'moonshot mentality' throughout the company allows people more freedom to find creative solutions as they attack problems with great passion."[7] Imagine what it must be like to work for Tesla or SpaceX right now. When the environment is created for innovation, everyone benefits because people feel meaning in being part of a leading movement. Innovation is not exclusive to high-tech companies. It exists in any business with the right mindset.

A healthy company culture requires authentic communication about what's really going on with staff, with customers, and with leadership. Building this level of trust is the basis of creating safety in the workplace and encouraging staff to take risks. If you want outside-the-box solutions or honest feedback at a bare minimum, a place for open dialogue is necessary.

If staff are ridiculed for their ideas or taunted or humiliated publicly or privately, people will shut down and not come forward with real feedback or creative ideas that might be the very thing the company needs to hear. Creating safety and trust has to start with the leadership if it's going to trickle down inside the company culture. "Teams that lack trust waste inordinate amounts of time and energy managing their behaviors and interactions within the group," says Lencioni. "They tend to dread team meetings and are reluctant to take risks in asking for or offering assistance to others. As a result, morale on distrusting teams is usually quite low, and unwanted turnover is high."[8] There's always a part of us scanning for safety in our environment, and if we don't feel it, this will shutdown productivity and innovation.

I once worked with a company that had an intimidating boss who would sometimes chew out her staff in front of others. You could hear her rants throughout the building. It created an atmosphere of blame and tension, as no one wanted to be the next person to get blasted. This resulted in an echo chamber around this leader; no one wanted to risk giving her feedback for fear of her reactions. The environment was filled with turmoil, as evidenced by the constantly rotating seats on the leadership team, which trickled down throughout the business.

On the flipside, leaders and managers who understand the importance of having everyone feel valued and respected will get more contribution and leadership from staff members. Having your team feel safe to share what needs to be shared without consequence or retaliation is the most important foundation for creating an innovative and forward-thinking atmosphere. Your team and colleagues won't come forward with their intuitive sense if there's not a real invitation for this. For example, it can be easy to say that you want feedback, but then get defensive when someone says something that goes against your self-image or perception.

There are an increasing number of software tools, such as Culture Amp or Know Your Company, from which you can get anonymous feedback from staff on their suggestions or level of engagement about anything in the business. Whether it's in group meetings or through occasional surveys, taking the temperature of your company culture is often an overlooked, yet critical feedback loop for healthy communication and team atmosphere.

One endearing way to bring more humility, humbleness, and openness into your company culture is for leaders to celebrate failures and to take ownership when things don't go as planned. This has the opposite effect of a blame culture, as everyone is encouraged to take ownership of their own flaws and imperfections. When leaders lead by example and can have levity and space around mistakes and failures, staff learn that there is room to not be perfect, that they can learn from make mistakes in a supportive environment, and that they can be more of themselves. This goes a long way in making it safe to take risks and fail, versus being risk-averse and maintaining the status quo, where no one learns and grows.

The more that leaders and managers are comfortable receiving everyone's ideas and feedback, the more encouragement and freedom people will feel to share. The more room there is for everyone to voice their opinions, to disagree yet listen to each other fully, and to have healthy conflict, the more trust you build for taking greater risks. Once you have established this level of safety and trust, you will get the most out of your people and their contribution to your strategic direction. Now you are ready to harness the power of your team and the freedom that they will feel to bring their intuitive knowing to the table. And this could be the very type of embodied insights that completely change the course of your company.

Encourage Intuition

Now that you have established a baseline of safety and trust to take risks on your team or within your company, the next step involves encouraging innovation and creative thinking. Igniting intuitive decision-making requires a balance between personal, reflective time, as well as bringing everyone together and harnessing the collective wisdom of the group. And as mentioned, the more you become the change that you want to see, the more people will follow your lead.

Whether it is for five minutes or three hours, personal time well spent is critical. Carving out solo time for slowing down, accessing your deeper subconscious mind, and approaching a situation from a fresh perspective is necessary for innovation. As strategic thinking accesses different parts of our brain, we need that time and space to sink deeper within ourselves and discover what's waiting for us. This means eliminating distractions, finding a suitable and inspiring environment, and allowing time to focus and go within. It's also important to encourage staff to make this quality time as well.

Once team members have made some time for personal reflection and clarity, it's incredibly powerful to bring everyone together to brainstorm and discuss strategy. There's a creative element that only happens in a collective field and people can bounce ideas off of each other. Doug Greene, founder of The New Hope Network whom we met back in Chapter 2, notes, "Intuition is fueled a great deal by who you are around. If you are around intuitive people, it can spark you like spark plugs and help you be more intuitive. It can help you open up feelings, channels, and things inside of you that by yourself you might not be able to access."[9]

If you know how to facilitate this space as a manager or leader, you will benefit from the wisdom and experience of the group. Staff members who feel included and respected are willing to give their best and contribute toward the greater good of the team. You can use some of the suggested exercises, such as the Embodied Decision-Making exercise in Chapter 6, to deepen intuitive decision-making as a group and truly harness the potential in the room for new ideas and solutions. These approaches will contribute to new breakthroughs that your team's critical thinking alone can't conceive.

Disrupt Your Routine

Interrupting typical patterns of thinking and helping your team get out of their heads is an effective way to bring intuition into your company culture. If you find yourself stuck or stagnant on the same problem and see no way around it, disrupt your typical routine or mode of thinking or that of your team's. This is why getting outside, stepping away from the computer, or engaging in a physical exercise or mindfulness practice can change your brain states and help you get into more of a flow state, in which you can access your subconscious creativity and intuition. Steven Kotler and Jamie Wheal, the founders of the Flow Genome Project, have dedicated themselves to this research and define "flow" as "optimal states of consciousness where we feel our best and perform our best."[10] When performers and high achievers describe being "in the zone," they are so focused in the moment and the task at hand that everything else disappears in the background.

Doug Greene has experienced the value of disrupting normal ways of thinking and getting staff out of their logical, rational minds since the 1980s. He was one of the trendsetters who would bring in trainers or jugglers, or take his team on field trips to intentionally get them out of their typical mindset. He was one of the first people to transform trade shows into events that involved music, dancing, and interactive classes to learn and deepen networks far more than a sterile business environment could do on its own. "I just found that if you could put people together in situations outside of their normal day-to-day routine in a positive situation, with a spirit of generosity and collaboration," says Doug, "they would take those seeds and grow them into their own innovations that we couldn't even imagine."[11]

Play is also a key disruptor and one that is often lacking in the business context. We accept the value of play as children, but we don't often appreciate how vital this is to business and decision-making as adults, in sparking the creativity, joy, and ingenuity of staff. "I have seen play help executives find new ideas and shape better teams, show more engagement, and reach higher levels of efficiency,"[12] says international business consultant and author Francis Cholle. "Play opens the doors to our deeper creative potential, helping us achieve change and implement innovative solutions."[13]

One business I work with offers improv classes as an option for learning how to intuit the moment and play off of other people in social dynamics. Translating improv classes into business has tremendous upsides. In fact, Chicago's famous Second City improv troupe has expanded to lead corporate trainings. Business schools at universities such as Duke and Stanford are including improv classes in their curriculum to help future leaders cope with a rapidly changing environment.[14] They have noticed that the staff leaves these classes feeling more confident, and they also think faster, embrace failure more easily, have increased awareness and listening skills, and learn how to read social dynamics and cues, which has directly related to their role in the company. By breaking up routine patterns and modes of thinking, you are creating space for individual and collective intuition and genius to flourish. Now let's look at how to assess the level of intuitive intelligence within your organization and how to make your company culture smarter.

Intuitive Engagement Pathway

Now that you followed the steps to create the right environment for intuition and innovation to thrive, how do you advance intuitive intelligence for your leaders and teams? The first step is to be able to assess how your organization is engaging with their intuitive intelligence today, and then identify what the next steps look like to advance this game-changing resource. One of the advantages of working with a wide variety of companies and industries around the world is witnessing the universal principles of what creates a culture of innovation versus one of stagnation. And I've seen plenty of both! From my direct experience and research, I've built an assessment tool called the Intuitive Engagement Pathway to help you identify where you and your company are at in terms of engaging with your own intuitive intelligence as a powerful resource for decision-making and communication (see Figure 5). The following six stages deepen your own relationship with your intuitive intelligence and activate this within your company culture for greater innovation.

1. **Awareness:** The first step on the journey of deepening your intuitive intelligence is to recognize its existence in the first place. Think back to certain hunches and instincts that you've felt in the past. The ones that you wish you'd listened to. This is your intuition. Once you connect the dots of examples from your past, you establish the first baseline of validity based on your own life experience.

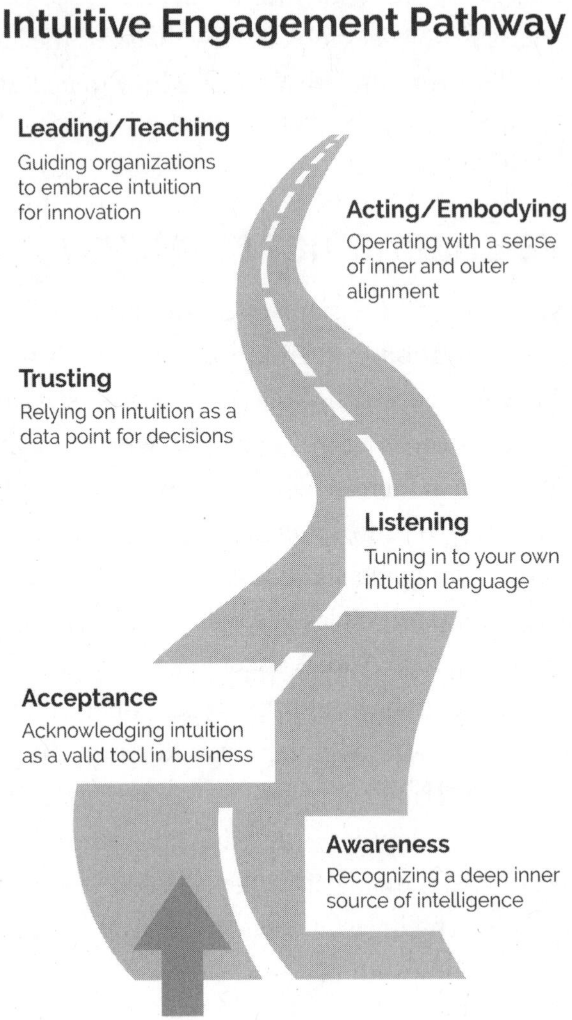

Intuitive Engagement Pathway

Leading/Teaching
Guiding organizations to embrace intuition for innovation

Acting/Embodying
Operating with a sense of inner and outer alignment

Trusting
Relying on intuition as a data point for decisions

Listening
Tuning in to your own intuition language

Acceptance
Acknowledging intuition as a valid tool in business

Awareness
Recognizing a deep inner source of intelligence

Figure 5.

2. **Acceptance:** You may be aware of intuition in a general sense, but it doesn't mean that you accept it as a valid tool in your business decision-making. This stage is about working through old conditioning and the five obstacles of intuition that get in the way of acknowledging and tuning in to your deeper source of intelligence. Once you accepted that your inner guidance is worth listening to and has real impact in your decision-making, gross skepticism and doubt fade away as you naturally strengthen the relationship with your intuitive center.

3. **Listening:** In this step, you learn to discover how your internal guidance system speaks to you, and continue to deepen the relationship with your intuition for more powerful decision-making in your organization. This is where it moves from general acceptance of intuition as a concept to a personal and experiential relationship as you learn how to distinguish the voice of your intuition from your inner critic, strong emotions, and other internal and external interference.

4. **Trusting:** Now that you developed a personal relationship with your intuition, it doesn't mean that you always trust it as a reliable source for decision-making when real pressures are on the line. This is where your relationship with intuition is truly tested. In fact, this is one of the primary stages in which we betray our inner knowing and often regret this later. This stage is about learning to trust what you feel and that you are picking up on valid, nuanced data all around you, all the time, to inform yourself to make the best decisions possible. Research, data, and analytics are imperative to reinforce your inner decision-making, but not to replace or cancel out your inner knowing.

5. **Acting/Embodying:** Acting on your gut instinct is the next step of an engaged relationship with your intuition. Action is what brings your innermost senses into reality in a practical way that changes the culture and course of your organization. When you live your life from this reference point, you are upleveling your ability to make more conscious, holistic, and well-rounded choices and strategy, instead of only coming from the limitations of the conscious, rational mind. This is where intuitive leadership is birthed.

6. **Teaching/Leading:** The final step of completion is the ability to encourage and foster intuitive intelligence within your teams and organization. It's about mentoring others to cultivate their deeper intelligence, which benefits their individual growth as well as a greater contribution to your organization. It's truly a win-win-win and the fastest route to embracing innovation. The leaders that are teaching this are creating the companies that people want to work for. And everyone benefits as a result.

Apply the Three Dimensions of Intuition Into Your Business

Lastly, let's look at how to implement the three dimensions of intuitive intelligence into your company culture.

Apply Directional Intuition

As introduced in Chapter 6, directional intuition is your "navigator." It's your internal feedback system, or your inner GPS that you have come equipped with, yet it may be rusty from neglect or lack of practice. Finding your own voice and listening to your inherent wisdom has never been more challenging with today's speed, outside noise, and information overload. Therefore, following the six steps to cultivate your intuition is the most effective practice to help you get in touch with your inner compass. By intentionally becoming more receptive, slowing down, differentiating from your doubts and critic, listening to the wisdom of your body, asking for guidance, and acting on your natural intelligence, you build an ongoing relationship with your intuitive intelligence. The more you practice refining your directional intuition, the more trustworthy this resource becomes as a real discernment tool in any decision or choice-point in business.

You will start to notice the subtle nuances of when you feel something "off" or "on the money" when it comes to key decision-making at work. By learning the language of your intuition (discussed in Chapter 1), you will get clearer on how your directional intuition speaks to you. It takes time to become fluent in this new language, yet when you make the time to establish this relationship, you will arrive at decisions more quickly and holistically. The most common applications of directional intuition in the workplace are strategic decision-making, brainstorming, innovation and break-through strategies, product development, entrepreneurial visioning, hiring, firing, and general organizational strategy; leadership and general business direction including partner dynamics, and marketing strategy; and assessing timing, such as product roll-outs. It can take the form of individual or group strategy sessions, leadership retreats, and structures that help you interrupt the conscious, rational mind and tune into your deeper intelligence.

For example, if the company is going in a certain direction and your gut is not aligned, it is a clear indicator that either you need to speak up and really debate it out, or maybe it's time for you to leave the company. When team members are not on board in a fundamental way and talking it through doesn't lead to a shared vision or resolution, it is often in the best interest of the individual and the company to move on.

By putting the exercises in this book into practice, you will gain new insights and creativity through inviting your staff to slow down and access their nonconscious minds and intuition. As Darcy Winslow observes from her own experience:

> *Test out intuitive thinking. Like anything that you are learning, you have to practice to develop it. It's very liberating to not be boundaried by traditional thinking. Change happens on the fringe. If you stay in the center and always do what you've always done, you always get what you've always gotten—just more of it. If you want something different, do something different. Tapping into that deep core of sensing and knowing—I think we need it now more than ever.*[15]

Most importantly, you are inviting the full contribution of all stakeholders to be part of key discussions and decisions that will impact the future of your organization. Everyone benefits from this participation. Jason Gore, who we met in Chapter 4, is a cofounder of Neuberg, Gore, and Associates and works primarily as an executive coach for newer generation leaders and startups. Gore, who is immersed in the latest trends, notes, "For most companies today, your people are your greatest assets. In a world where the most innovative companies win, leaders who listen to their intuition as part of their decision process are leading the charge. Intuition is essential for all the micro-choices that allow one innovation to succeed while another fails."[16]

On the biggest picture level, your directional intuition helps you align your work with your highest aspirations in your life, no matter where you sit on the chart. It represents the "true north" of your direction and purpose. When your values and motivations are in alignment with your directional intuition, you will notice a natural passion that comes through without forcing anything. Work may seem effortless even though there still may be long hours that are full of challenges. Connecting to your passion and purpose provides an incredible fuel source. You might also experience that you are in a state of flow where life seems to be supporting your actions when you are in alignment in this bigger way and you have moved beyond what is simply convenient or comfortable. You are moving toward what is most fulfilling.

Apply Social Intuition

Social intuition is your "vibe detector." It's the aspect of your intuition that helps you sense and read people and interpersonal interactions in your environment, which predominantly consists of the energies and emotions in the room. Social intuition is based on a combination of emotional intelligence, nonverbal communication, social dynamics, presence, body language, cues, and the congruence and dissonance of what people are expressing and not expressing.

Training your team to develop their social intuition creates an immediate impact in leadership, management, sales, customer service, marketing, group decision-making, investment pitching, presenting, negotiating, navigating conflict, and any aspect of business that has a relational component. It allows for a higher level of communication and the ability to adapt to change, both internally as well as with customers. The ability to read nonverbal communication and social dynamics lead to a smarter company culture that outperforms and innovates beyond the competition.[17] Unfortunately, the ability to intuit the needs of your team and customer base is all too uncommon.

McKinsey conducted a survey and found that more than 70 percent of senior executives said that innovation is one of the top three drivers of growth in their companies and that executives see innovation as the most important way to accelerate the pace of change in today's global business environment.[18] The key finding in the research also showed that two-thirds of senior executives were not confident in how to stimulate and inspire innovation with their teams. While 94 percent of executives surveyed know that people and culture are the key to innovation, they haven't developed the required skills to impact their team in an innovative and effective way.

As Steven Rogall, CEO of Rogall Painting whom we met in Chapter 3, reflects:

At the end of the day, the most complex thing that you are going to deal with are the people that you lead. You inherit everything they bring to the table and it's not just the degree that they hang on your wall. It's all the stuff in their life.

Your job is to see and develop them. When you start hearing things like, 'Man, I'm growing as a person for having been here,' that's a mark of a good manager. Companies that don't develop their people will end up losing in the long run. Especially nowadays as the generational shifts happen, you can't lead a company without dealing with some of these subjects. You will become obsolete. No one is going to want to work for you. That's what it comes down to.[19]

Steven is speaking to the necessity for leaders and managers to possess and cultivate their own emotional intelligence and social intuition in order to develop their teams. This is one of the key differentiators for company cultures to thrive and a boon for businesses that get this. When staff are motivated, engaged, and inspired toward innovation, not only do people want to work there, but customers also feel this on the other side.

According to a McKinsey research study in which they surveyed 600 managers on innovation and leadership, they concluded that the top three inhibitors of innovation were leaders who pay lip service to it but don't do anything about it, leaders who don't encourage innovative behavior such as risk-taking and openness to new ideas, and rewarding only short-term performance and maintaining a fear of failure.[20] This is one of the key reasons why employee engagement is scored so low annually.

The Gallup 2017 State of the American Workplace reports that only 33 percent of employees feel engaged at work.[21] Disengaged employees "are more likely to steal from their company, negatively influence their coworkers, miss workdays, and drive customers away."[22] Gallup estimates that actively disengaged employees cost the US $483 billion to $605 billion each year in lost productivity.

Companies who develop social intuition with their staff can literally save millions of dollars and have the clear edge over companies that don't, as they can spot toxic work dynamics before they get out of hand.

Social intuition inside most company cultures is severely lacking, often because there is not enough attention and investment put on its development. Companies who invest in their people through embracing such training and implementation lead to high-performance environments that people want to work for. Companies like GlassDoor.com have now made it easier to peek into a company culture and read candid reviews of employees' experience. In today's world, you can't hide anymore, which makes it a necessity to proactively work on developing the emotional intelligence and intuitive nature of your team. Developing social intuition is no longer an option if you are serious about effective communication, increased ability to adapt to change, and deepening relationships, all forming a stronger and smarter company culture.

In a culture of health, employee well-being and organizational success are inextricably linked. This is why I recommend taking a company culture health audit. You can assess the level of a company's overall health and social intuition in order to make recommendations and plan for how to increase the level of functioning as a highly effective team. As the 2017 Gallup poll clearly states, "Employees who are engaged are more likely to stay with their organization, reducing overall turnover and the costs associated with it. They feel a stronger bond to their organization's mission and purpose, making them more effective brand ambassadors. They build stronger relationships with customers, helping their company increase sales and profitability."[23]

When you can focus on your company or department's struggles when it comes to adaptive leadership, trust, team work, employee engagement, and feeling good about the organization as a whole, you can make the greatest gains in transforming your company culture immediately. As the business world continues to get the value of authentic communication and its relevance to employee buy-in, engagement, innovation, and fulfillment, this trend will only increase.

One of the most exciting opportunities for growth in this sector is the fact that you can build and train emotional intelligence, nonverbal communication, the ability to navigate conflict, improve listening skills, strengthen leadership and team dynamics, and develop social intuition skills with your company culture. From management to sales, these skills can be applied to any relational component of the business.

As the business world continues to embrace softer skills around emotional intelligence and communication, social intuition will continue to increase in company cultures, providing for a smarter team that knows how to work together and better adapt to change. Working on your own "vibe detector" increases with self-awareness, personal development, and learning how to tune into body language and nonverbal communication, and will benefit you in any position in the business.

Apply Informational Intuition

As a refresher from Chapter 1, informational intuition is the ability to synthesize large amounts of data and decode information rapidly for analysis, pattern recognition, and decision-making.

I call it "the integrator." This skill involves rapidly recognizing patterns and analyzing information and experiences—including those stored in the subconscious mind. This is one of the most valuable skills that an employee can possess because they become unconsciously competent in their field and see what others can't see, naturally. In some ways, informational intuition is the hardest one to teach. One of the key factors to building this skill is becoming a master of your craft. The more you study the stock market, data science, the behaviors of infants in the critical care unit of a nursery,[24] or whatever industry you are in, you will naturally intuit patterns based on your experience and identify the data points that are stored in your nonconscious mind.

Cheskie Weisz, CEO of CW Realty Management, specializes in real estate property management and development headquartered in Brooklyn, New York. Cheskie built his business on trusting his gut sense and using informational intuition to know the exact value of a building. For example, he can intuit the buildable square footage value, the potential income, and the price-per-foot for rent.

Without looking at spreadsheets of data, Cheskie can quote you on the square foot value of a new apartment unit on the corner of Van Brunt and Verona in the Red Hook neighborhood of Brooklyn, and how that value changes if a credit union or Starbucks opens next door. Imagine all of the calculations that factor into the changing dynamics of a neighborhood!

Informational intuition comes with experience. It comes with pattern recognition of knowing your industry, your market, your products, and services over a given time. You are able to take complex sets of data and arrive at accurate conclusions in seconds.

Cheskie says, "If you can't get the value of a building within seconds of walking into it, you are in the wrong business."[25] He has people on his team that verify his gut sense with number-crunching, yet imagine how much time he saves his company in decision-making.

Informational intuition comes from "going all in" on your craft. "When I meet a buyer or seller, I can tell within minutes if there's a deal to be made," says Cheskie. "There's no college course that will teach you that if a deli opens up on the corner and people eat outside, that no one will buy a condominium right next door."[26] He observes that banks are limited because they have their formulas for price-per-square-foot or price-per-door, but in reality, there are some things you can't find on a spreadsheet. This should not be the only factor in making a decision if you should buy or not buy. "That's where you need to rely on that gut intuition on the price of what you can sell for, no matter what the piece of paper says. The real money is in the feel of the situation."[27]

One aspect of informational intuition is in developing the skills to know what questions to ask next, or how to interpret the data in the first place. "When hypotheses are proposed, individuals intuitively decide whether they are worth trying to prove or refute. Intuition also helps them decide where to look for facts, how to design experiments, and how to interpret data and recognize what is relevant,"[28] says Philip Goldberg in *The Intuitive Edge*. This developed skill is an incredible asset in business, as you know where to focus your attention, which questions to ask, and how to mobilize your team on searching the right data that gives you the feedback and projections you are after.

Cate Harding[29] knows this first hand. She is the director of customer insights at a Silicon Valley consumer technology company.

211

Her team focuses on researching and predicting consumer trends in retail and online, as well as measuring internal employee satisfaction. They research three to four big topics a year, and Cate needs to trust her intuition on which topics are worth exploring, such as how Millennials use technology, or how the workplace is changing.

One value that is appreciated at her company is the ability to anticipate the future and "see around corners." She says this is something that is encouraged and talked about a lot. This is part of why the company has been a leader in innovation for decades. Relying on her intuition regarding what to research has saved Cate's company incredible amounts of time because she is not encumbered by analysis paralysis, which often plagues the research field in general.

Cate has learned to apply informational intuition in a highly skilled way: She marries her reliance on intuition with her passion for data. She uses intuition to feel into what trends to research, vigorously analyzes the data, and then uses intuition again on how to interpret the story that the data is telling her. "Using your intuition is a short-hand. You have to sense the bigger story and the call to action. You end up with 1,000 data points and you need to be able to rely on your intuition to comprehend 'what's the story we are telling out of this?'"[30] The challenge, as Cate articulates, is learning how to slice the data, which is a key element to informational intuition. "The problem is that there is so much data that it's overwhelming. Looking at a particular cut of data or cutting the data a certain way, one has to use intuition in the story you are interpreting."[31]

Cate shows us how analytics and intuition can co-exist in a powerful way. In fact, she intuits that with the advent of AI, the necessity of human intuition will be more important than ever. "With artificial intelligence, you are going to be able to crunch everything. Intuition is what the machine doesn't have. What's going to become most prized and valuable is our human intuition because that will point the machine in the right direction," says Cate. "You'll have this perfect assistant that will grab you anything you want. But how you direct and focus that assistant makes all the difference." Lastly, she states, "We are going to have to double-down on the creativity of the human being. It's a right-brainer's era to come. Not a left brainer's era. We are coming into an era where intuition is that much more important and is what needs to be developed to balance Big Data."[32] Besides excelling at your craft and gaining experience to better recognize patterns and trends, informational intuition can also be developed through accelerated learning and memorization techniques, as well as speed reading and accessing your subconscious mind through hypnosis, NLP, and other mediums. All of these modalities help at arriving at faster decision-making and learning how to extract the essence of complex patterning.

Conclusion

Implementing directional, social, and informational intuition in business are what separates you from the pack. When all three are applied throughout the different sectors of your business, it gives you the invisible edge over companies that don't. This is one of the most direct ways to up-level your team in terms of innovation and creativity. Hopefully, this book has opened your eyes to new areas of possibility regarding tapping into the human potential on your teams and in your business. This most important asset, when paid attention to and developed, will ensure that you stay on the leading edge of your field and industry as you harness the collective wisdom of your people.

It has to start with you. Following the main practices of this book will help you cultivate your directional intuition and inner guidance, which will enable you to apply this in social and informational contexts. In review, the six steps in order are:

1. **Become more receptive.** This first step is all about setting the foundation by shifting your orientation to an open one in which you allow information to come toward you. You will need to suspend the judging mind and simply collect all the data that is coming toward you each second. This is where you move from "doing" to "being" and allow your intuition to find you.

2. **Slow down.** This stage is critical in allowing yourself to still your mind from the speed and noise of your thoughts and the busyness of the outer world, so that you can get present to the moment. This is where the quiet voice of your intuition can find you.

3. **Separate from your inner critic.** Once you slow down, you'll often hear the voice of your inner critic get louder and distract you from the voice of your intuition. Learning how to get separation from the voice of your critic is paramount. You can learn to recognize the natural notes and tones of your inner guidance—then you will no longer be misled by the seduction of the critic's familiar narratives, which are based on the past.

Now you are ready to tune into what's happening in the present moment without distraction.

4. **Listen to your body.** Once you have separated from the inner critic, you can identify the voice of your inner knowing and wisdom, and have greater discernment that you are in alignment with this source. Now you can drop in deeper to listen to what your signals and cues are telling you through the body and your subconscious mind.

5. **Ask for guidance.** Through decoding your intuitive language, you develop an intimate relationship with your tuning fork by asking a question that's present for you in the business, and then listening to your response based on the language of your inner guidance.

6. **Act on your inner intelligence.** The last step that really anchors your intuition into reality is taking action on what you feel. This is where change happens. This takes commitment and courage to follow your "true north" and be willing to go against the grain in order to stand for the deeper wisdom that lives inside of you. Bringing your feelings into action is the birthplace of true creativity, possibility, and innovation.

Through practicing all of these steps, you are forging a new foundation and relationship with yourself. This takes time to really slow down and recognize how your intuition speaks to you, to develop an authentic relationship that you can trust by testing it out over time, and by putting this into action to make a dynamic impact and follow the leadership beat of your own drum. Through this commitment, you will find that this is one of the greatest gifts in your life as you have a true inner ally that is there to support you when business decisions or life dilemmas look uncertain, chaotic, or stressful.

Once your directional intuition is strengthened, your social and informational intuition will be taken to new heights and depths. It is rare that someone excels at all three forms of intuition. Often you will find that you have a natural inclination in one or two of these intuitive skill sets. Know your superpower while also working on rounding out what might not come as naturally to you. For example, if you are great at listening to your directional intuition for key decisions in business, but don't feel like you have a read on your people or customers, then it's worth building your social intuition skills. Or if informational intuition comes to you intrinsically, but you don't know how to make decisions with the information you gather, then working on your directional intuition will be an incredible asset. I recommend developing your intuitive skills through the practices mentioned in this book, as well as hiring those around you to round out what you may lack. In other words, play to your strengths, keep developing your self-awareness and intuition, and hire top talent around you to support this higher-level intelligence throughout your company culture.

The more you practice the six steps in regards to developing a relationship with your intuition, the more this will change how you relate to the choices you make in business and in life. From my own personal experience with those I have interviewed, researched, worked with, and spoken to around the world, people who listen to, trust, and take action from their inner guidance feel more on-purpose and fulfilled than those who don't. It's a great feeling to be able to trust yourself on the deepest of levels when it comes to decision-making, reading out the environment around you, and to integrate large amounts of information quickly. This is an empowering step in bringing more of yourself to your decision-making at work and in life, and I'm confident that this will result in greater access to your inherent creativity, innovation, and ability to listen to the deeper thread in your life that serves your purpose and impacts those around you. I look forward to hearing what you discover!

NOTES

Introduction

1. Daniel Goleman, *Emotional Intelligence: Why It Can Matter More than IQ* (New York: Bantam Books, 1997).

2. Andrew McAfee, "Managerial Intuition Is a Harmful Myth," *Harvard Business Review*, February 8, 2012, *https://hbr. org/2012/02/managerial-intuition-is-a-harm.html*.

3. Daniel Kahneman, *Thinking, Fast and Slow* (New York: Farrar, Straus and Giroux, 2011), 212.

4. Ibid., 103.

5. Richard Branson, *Losing My Virginity: How I've Survived, Had Fun, and Made a Fortune Doing Business My Way* (New York: Crown Business, 1998), 190.

6. Oprah Winfrey, "What Oprah Knows for Sure About Trusting Her Intuition," *O, The Oprah Magazine,* August 2011, *http://www.oprah.com*

7. Marissa Levin, "Why Google, Nike, and Apple Love Mindfulness Training, and How You Can Easily Love it Too," *Inc.,* June 12, 2017, *https://www.inc.com*

8. Gerard P. Hodgkinson, Eugene Sadler-Smith, Lisa A. Burke, Guy Claxton, and Paul R. Sparrow, "Intuition in Organizations: Implications for Strategic Management," *Long Range Planning* 42 (2009): 277–297.

Chapter 1

1. Nelia Joubert, interview with the author, April 13, 2017.

2. Marc David, interview with the author, May 6, 2017.

3. Malcolm Gladwell, *Blink: The Power of Thinking Without Thinking* (New York: Little, Brown, 2005), 11.

4. Ibid., 23.

5. Daniel Caruana, interview with the author, April 20, 2017.

6. Annie Jacobsen, "The U.S. Military Believes People Have a Sixth Sense," *Time,* April 3, 2017, *http://time.com/4721715/phenomena-annie-jacobsen/*

7. Ibid.

8. Mark Divine, *The Way of the SEAL: Think Like an Elite Warrior to Lead and Succeed* (White Plains, NY: Reader's Digest, 2013), 134.

9. Ibid., 134–135.

10. David Derbyshire, "Each Person Is Inundated With 174 Newspapers' Worth of Information EVERY DAY via Television, Emails and Post," DailyMail.com, February 11, 2011, *http://www.dailymail.co.uk/sciencetech/article-1355892/Each-person-inundated-174-newspapers-worth-information-EVERY-DAY.html*

Chapter 2

1. Daniel Caruana, interview with the author, April 20, 2017.

2. Doug Greene, interview with the author, November 1, 2017.

3. Silvia Belleza, Neeru Paharia, and Anat Keinan, "Research: Why Americans Are So Impressed by Busyness," *Harvard Business Review,* December 15, 2016, *https://hbr.org/2016/12/research-why-americans-are-so-impressed-by-busyness*

4. Doug Ramsay, "UC San Diego Experts Calculate How Much Information Americans Consume," UC San Diego News Center,

December 2009, *http://ucsdnews.ucsd.edu/archive/newsrel/ general/12-09Information.asp.*

5. J. S. Rubinstein, D. E. Meyer, and J. E. Evans, "Executive Control of Cognitive Processes in Task Switching," *Journal of Experimental Psychology: Human Perception and Performance* 27 (2001): 763–797

6. Neale Walsch, "Your Life Begins at the End of Your Comfort Zone," YouTube video, 1:58, posted by "ConsciousLivingDublin," October 5, 2011, *https://www.youtube.com/ watch?v=wQzDFjWPyf8*

7. Clayton Christiensen, *The Innovator's Dilemma: When New Technologies Cause Great Firms to Fail* (Brighton, MA: Harvard Business School Press), 1997.

8. Sherilee Joe, interview with the author, October 26, 2017.

9. Ibid.

10. Ibid.

11. Stephan Rechtschaffen, interview with the author, June 26, 2017.

Chapter 3

1. Lisa Dion, interview with the author, April 28, 2017.

2. "Table 7: Survival of Private Sector Establishments by Opening Year," U.S. Bureau of Labor Statistics, *https://www.bls.gov/bdm/ us_age_naics_00_table7.txt*

3. John McDermott, "Report: 75% of Venture-backed Start-ups Fail," *Inc.*, September 20, 2012, *https://www.inc.com*

4. Abraham Maslow, *The Psychology of Science* (New York: Harper & Row, 1966), 15.

5. Alexandra Rucki, "Average Smartphone User Checks Device 221 Times a Day, According to Research," *The Evening Standard*, October 7, 2014, *http://www.standard.co.uk/news/techandgad gets/average-smartphone-user-checks-device-221-times-a-day -according-to-research-9780810.html*

6. Steven Rogal, interview with the author, May 2, 2017.

7. Marc David, interview with the author, May 6, 2017.

8. David Gosse, "Transcript of Simon Sinek Millennials in the Workplace Interview," December 2016, *http://ochen.com*

9. Steven Rogall, interview with the author, May 2, 2017.

Chapter 4

1. Mike Orlando, interview with the author, April 20, 2017.

2. Ibid.

3. Ibid.

4. Carl Honoré, *In Praise Of Slow: How a Worldwide Movement Is Challenging the Cult of Speed* (London: Orion, 2005).

5. John Pencavel, "The Productivity of Working Hours," Discussion Paper No. 8129 (Stanford University and IZA, 2014).

6. Steven Kotler and Jamie Wheal, *Stealing Fire: How Silicon Valley, the Navy SEALs, and Maverick Scientists Are Revolutionizing the Way We Live and Work* (New York: HarperCollins, 2017).

7. David G. Myers, "Power and Perils of Intuition: Understanding the Nature of Our Gut Instincts, *The Scientific American* (2007): 24–31.

8. Ibid., 28–29.

9. T. Norretranders, *The User Illusion: Cutting Consciousness Down to Size* (New York: Penguin Books, 1998).

10. Bruce Lipton, *The Biology of Belief 10th Anniversary Edition: Unleashing the Power of Consciousness, Matter & Miracles* (Carlsbad, CA: Hay House, 2005).

11. Darcy Winslow, interview with the author, June 6, 2017.

12. Slade Machamer, interview with the author, Dec. 19, 2017.

13. Ibid.

14. Ibid.

15. Michael Harris, "Neuroscience Proves: Why We Buy on Emotion and Justify With Logic—But With a Twist," *Medium,* May 29, 2015, *https://medium.com/@salesforce/neuroscience-proves-we-buy-on-emotion-and-justify-with-logic-but-with-a-twist-4ff965cdeed8*

16. Jason Gore, interview with the author, July 24, 2017.

Chapter 5

1. Jonathan Raymond, interview with the author, January 9, 2018.

2. Carl Richards, "Learning to Deal With the Impostor Syndrome," *New York Times,* October 26, 2015.

3. Mesha Joy Machamer, interview with the author, February 8, 2018.

4. Ibid.

5. Ibid.

6. Bruce Lipton, T*he Biology of Belief, 10th Anniversary Edition: Unleashing the Power of Consciousness, Matter & Miracles.* (Carlsbad, CA: Hay House, 2005), 128.

7. Interview with Mesha Joy Machamer on February 8, 2018.

8. Ibid.

Chapter 6

1. Deborah Bowman, interview with the author, March 28, 2017.

2. Deborah Bowman, "Falling Into Grace," TEDx Talks, 9:37, posted by TEDx Talks, November 11, 2014, *https://www.you tube.com*

3. Deborah Bowman, interview with the author, March 28, 2017.

4. Grant Soosalu and Marvin Oka, *mBraining: Using Your Multiple Brains to Do Cool Stuff* (mBit International Pty. Ltd., 2012), 23.

5. Ibid., 10.

6. J. Andrew Armour, *Neurocardiology—Anatomical and Functional Principles* (University of Montreal, 1991).

7. Grant Soosalu and Marvin Oka, *mBraining: Using Your Multiple Brains to Do Cool Stuff* (mBit International Pty. Ltd., 2012), 26.

8. Dr. Michael Gershon, *The Second Brain: Your Gut Has a Mind of Its Own* (New York: HarperCollins, 1998).

9. Dan Hurley, "Your Backup Brain," *Psychology Today,* November/December 2011, accessed February 3, 2018, *http://www.psychologytoday.com/articles/201110/your-backup-brain*

10. Byron Robinson, *The Abdominal and Pelvic Brain: With Automatic Visceral Ganglia* (Chicago: Byron Robinson, 1907).

11. Grant Soosalu and Marvin Oka, *mBraining: Using Your Multiple Brains to Do Cool Stuff* (mBit International Pty. Ltd., 2012), 34.

12. Ibid., 47.

13. David Myers, *Intuition: Its Powers and Perils* (New Haven, CT: Yale University, 2002), 18.

14. Ibid., 20.

15. Gerard P. Hodgkinson, Eugene Sadler-Smith, Lisa A. Burke, Guy Claxton, and Paul R. Sparrow, "Intuition in Organizations: Implications for Strategic Management," *Long Range Planning* 42 (2009): 277–297.

16. A. B. Satpute and M. D. Lieberman, "Integrating Automatic and Controlled Processes Into Neurocognitive Models of Social Cognition," *Brain Research* 1079 (2006): 86–97.

17. Gerard P. Hodgkinson, Eugene Sadler-Smith, Lisa A. Burke, Guy Claxton, and Paul R. Sparrow, "Intuition in Organizations: Implications for Strategic Management," *Long Range Planning* 42 (2009): 286.

18. Candace Pert, *Molecules of Emotion: The Science Behind Mind -Body Medicine* (New York: Touchstone, 1997).

19. Lisa Dion, interview with the author, April 28, 2017.

20. M. Szegedy-Maszak, "Mysteries of the Mind: Your Unconscious Is Making Your Everyday Decisions," *US News and World Report* 28 no. 2 (2005): 53–61.

21. Bruce H. Lipton, "Who's Driving Your Karma, Anyway? How Your Subconscious Mind Runs the Show," HealYourLife.com, May 25, 2014, accessed February 10, 2018, *https://www.healy ourlife.com/who-s-driving-your-karma-anyway*

22. Bruce Lipton, *The Biology of Belief, 10th Anniversary Edition: Unleashing the Power of Consciousness, Matter & Miracles* (Carlsbad, CA: Hay House, 2005).

23. Bruce Lipton, "The Power of the Mind," *New Dawn Magazine,* January 1, 2008, accessed February 14, 2018, *https://www. newdawnmagazine.com/articles/the-power-of-the-mind*

24. Brené Brown, *The Gifts of Imperfection: Let Go of Who You Think You're Supposed to Be and Embrace Who You Are* (Center City, MN: Hazelden Publishing, 2010), 70.

25. Tom Pepple, interview with the author, April 10, 2017.

26. Ibid.

27. Edward L. Bernays, "The Museum of Public Relations," YouTube video, 2:03, posted by "SpectorPR," April 5, 2011, *https://www. youtube.com/watch?time_continue=123&v=KLudEZpMjKU*

28. Ibid.

29. Ibid.

30. Scott Swanson, interview with the author, December 28, 2017.

31. Ibid.

Chapter 7

1. Michael Lacey, interview with the author, April 13, 2017.

2. Michael Lacey, interview with the author, February 22, 2018.

3. Lillian T. Eby, Tammy D. Allen, Sarah C. Evans, Thomas Ng, David DuBois, "Does Mentoring Matter? A Multidisciplinary

Meta-Analysis Comparing Mentored and Non-Mentored Individuals," *The National Center for Biotechnology Information* 72 (April 2008): 2, accessed February 21, 2018, *https://www.ncbi.nlm.nih.gov/pmc/articles/PMC2352144/*

4. Gary Klein, *The Power Of Intuition: How to Use Your Gut Feelings to Make Better Decisions at Work* (New York: Doubleday), 2002.

5. Ibid., 16.

6. Scott Swanson, interview with the author, December 28, 2017.

7. Bernadette Jiwa, *Hunch: Turn Your Everyday Insights Into the Next Big Thing* (New York: Portfolio/Penguin, 2017), 20.

8. Ibid., 15.

9. Brené Brown, *Daring Greatly: How the Courage to Be Vulnerable Transforms the Way We Live, Love, Parent, and Lead* (New York: Penguin, 2012).

Chapter 8

1. Darcy Winslow, interview with the author, June 6, 2017.

2. Ibid.

3. Darcy Winslow, interview with the author, December 22, 2017.

4. Ibid.

5. *http://www.academyforchange.org/*

6. Sheena Iyengar and Mark Lepper, "When Choice Is Demotivating: Can One Desire Too Much of a Good Thing?," *Journal of Personality and Social Psychology* 79 (2000): 6, accessed March 15, 2018, *https://faculty.washington.edu/jdb/345/345%20Articles/Iyengar%20%26%20Lepper%20(2000).pdf*

7. Jayson Gaddis, interview with the author, May 11, 2017.

8. Ibid.

9. Micha Mikailian, interview with the author, May 31, 2017.

10. Ibid.

11. Ibid.

12. Cate Stephenson, interview with the author, May 10, 2017.

13. Ibid.

14. Darcy Winslow, interview with the author, June 6, 2017.

Chapter 9

1. Patrick Lencioni, *The Advantage: Why Organizational Health Trumps Everything Else in Business* (San Francisco: Jossey-Bass, 2012), 37.

2. Lisa Dion, interview with the author, April 28, 2017.

3. Julia Rozovsky, "The Five Keys to a Successful Google Team," *Work,* November 17, 2015, accessed March 29, 2018. *https://rework.withgoogle.com/blog/five-keys-to-a-successful-google-team/*

4. Jim Oakley, interview with the author, May 5, 2017.

5. Ibid.

6. Alissa Newcomb and Jo Ling Kent, "'Google Manifesto' Firing Highlights What You Can and Can't Say at Work," NBC News, August 8, 2017, accessed March 29, 2018, *https://www. nbcnews.com/tech/tech-news/google-manifesto-highlights-what -you-can-can-t-say-work-n790981*

7. Jim Oakley, interview with the author, May 5, 2017.

8. Patrick Lencioni, *The Five Dysfunctions of a Team: A Leadership Fable* (San Francisco: Jossey-Bass, 2002), 196.

9. Doug Greene, interview with the author, November 1, 2017.

10. Steven Kotler and Jamie Wheal, *Stealing Fire: How Silicon Valley, the Navy SEALs, and Maverick Scientists Are Revolutionizing the Way We Live and Work* (New York: HarperCollins, 2017), 4.

11. Doug Greene, interview with the author, November 1, 2017.

12. Francis Cholle, *The Intuitive Compass: Why the Best Decisions Balance Reason and Instinct* (San Francisco: Jossey-Bass, 2012), 3.

13. Ibid.

14. Samantha White, "How an Improv Class Can Help Develop Essential Business Skills," *Financial Management*, February 1, 2018, accessed March 10, 2018, *https://www.fm-magazine.com/ issues/2018/feb/improv-class-helps-develop-business-skills.html*

15. Darcy Winslow, interview with the author, June 6, 2017.

16. Jason Gore, interview with the author, July 24, 2017.

17. Harvey Deutschdorf, "Why Emotionally Intelligent People Are More Successful," *Fast Company*, June 22, 2015, accessed March 15, 2018, *https://www.fastcompany.com/3047455/why -emotionally-intelligent-people-are-more-successful*

18. Joanna Barsh, Marla M. Capozzi, and Jonathan Davidson, "Leadership and Innovation," *McKinsey & Company*, January 2008, accessed March 9, 2018, *https://www.immagic.com*

19. Steven Rogall, interview with the author, May 2, 2017.

20. Joanna Barsh, Marla M. Capozzi, and Jonathan Davidson, "Leadership and Innovation," *McKinsey & Company*, January 2008, accessed March 9, 2018, *https://www.immagic.com*

21. "State of the American Workplace," Gallup, 2017, accessed March 18, 2018.

22. Ibid., 19.

23. Ibid., 19.

24. Gary Klein, *The Power of Intuition: How to Use Your Gut Feelings to Make Better Decisions at Work* (New York: Doubleday), 2002.

25. Cheskie Weisz, interview with the author, January 24, 2018.

26. Ibid.

27. Ibid.

28. Philip Goldberg, *The Intuitive Edge: Understanding Intuition and Applying It in Everyday Life* (Lincoln, NE: Backpinprint. com, 2006), 22.

29. Cate Harding, interview with the author, June 20, 2017.

30. Ibid.

31. Ibid.

32. Ibid.

Acknowledgments

It takes a village to write a book, and I'm blown away by all of the people who came together at the right time to help usher this one into existence.

To my literary agent, Jill Marsal, thank you for believing in me and in this work. I appreciate how quickly you helped this book find its home. To my publisher, Michael Pye, and the whole team at Red Wheel/Weiser. Thank you for taking a chance on a first-time author and trusting your intuition that the ideas in this book need to get in front of the right audience.

A special thank you to Stuart Horowitz, who helped guide me in the earliest stages, from concept to structure, and showed me what it takes to write a book. Your editing, feedback, and perspective were invaluable.

I also had the help and support of some key friends who brought incredible expertise and insight in making these chapters better. Thank you to David Coates, Jill Stacey, Mesha Machamer, and Sarah Hopkinson for your generous contributions. I also want to thank Brett Valley for your encouragement and help in teasing out the thread of this book in the very early stages.

I especially want to thank all of the business owners and managers whom I interviewed for this book. Hearing your stories of how you bring intuition into your everyday lives made this book come alive in a whole new way. I learned so much from these exchanges and appreciate you each taking the time out of your busy days to share your wisdom and experience.

I want to thank my business clients whom I get the honor of working with and putting these theories into practice. It is humbling that you each have that inner spark to create something better, and that you are not trying to do it all alone. A great model for me and many others.

Lastly, I want to thank my family, who have been with me through the highs and lows. I love you and appreciate all of the support you've given for me to find my own way.

To my amazing community of heartful and soulful friends around the world who have helped inspire my gifts to come forward and whom I salute in making this world a more conscious and connected place. Our work is just getting started.

I also want to thank Céline and Steve for helping make my writing retreat villa in France a real home. This whole process started to anchor when you welcomed me into your family and space.

Lastly, lastly, I want to acknowledge you, the reader. Thank you for taking the time to read these words. What I'm most excited about is to see what you do with them. I can't wait to hear your stories of locating your inner guidance in more moments of the day, and how this impacts your life and the lives of those around you.

INDEX

acceptance, intuitive engagement pathway and, 201

acting and the intuitive engagement pathway, 202

adaptability and intuition, 6

adaptive leadership, 41, 142, 185–186
struggles with, 209

advisor, benefits of having an, 157

analysis paralysis, 177–178

anxiety and social media, 67

artificial intelligence, 5

asking powerful questions, 161–162

asking yourself a question, the benefits of, 74

authenticity and intuition, 56

awareness, intuitive engagement pathway and, 199

befriending your inner critic, 105–126

behavior, predicting future, 7

beta brain wave states, slowing down your, 89

biases, letting go of implicit, 66

biases of intuition, 4

blame culture, 195

body,
benefits of moving your, 73

listening to your, 10, 127–150, 215

neural networks throughout the, 134

body language
and your inner critic, 119

in business, 27

breathing, the benefits of deep, 73

business and intuition, 3

business decisions, gut sense and, 191

business meetings, receptivity and, 79

busyness and intuition, 46–50

cells, neural receptors and the body's, 138

challenges of listening to intuition, 38

change, the inner critic and fear of, 117

clients, trouble-making, 74–75

coach, benefits of having a, 157

comfort zone and doubt, your, 43

comfort zone,
creating a, 51–52

staying in your, 29

commitment, 182–185
the importance of, 182–183

communication breakdown, clients and, 74–75

company culture,
leaders and, 190

making a smarter, 189–217

compassion as a soft skill, 3

confidence, subjective, 4

confirmation bias, the inner critic and, 113

conflict, navigating, 209

confrontation, learning to block out, 143

confrontations and creating space, 79

conscious mind,
environmental stimuli and the, 90

exercising and the, 101

fear and the, 51

conscious mind stream, slowing down from your, 91

conscious rational mind, valuing our, 142

consciousness, accessing your deeper, 90

conversation,
     slowing down the, 94
     inner guidance and, 29

core identity of self, 55

core negative beliefs, the inner critic and, 115

courage, 179–182

creating space, 77–78

creating space and confrontations, 79

creative thinking, encouraging, 196

creativity, creating an atmosphere of, 193

critic, befriending your inner, 105–126

critical thinking and intuition, 5

critical voice, active, 109

data, informational intuition and, 5, 24

data and intuition, 146

day-to-day business decisions, 20–21

dead-end job, staying in a, 177

decision-making,
     embodied, 147–150
     hesitation in, 177–178
     inner guidance and, 29
     leaders and, 192

decision-making
     abilities, trusting your, 159
     and fear, 51
     and intuition, 6, 143–144
     power, taking ownership of, 38

decisions,
     day-to-day business, 20–21
     slowing down and making better, 89–90

decisions and momentum, 181–182

Digital Age, the, 5

digital technology, the inundation of, 29

dimensions of intuition, three, 20–25

divine nature, guidance from your, 21

directional intuition, 20–22, 157–160
     applying, 202–205
     integrating, 26–31
     and inner guidance, 157

disrupting your routine, 197–199

distractions, eliminating, 65

distrust in yourself, doubt and, 43–44

doubt
     and intuition, 42–46
     and the inner critic, 110

ego and intuition, 54–59

electronic devices, turning off your, 72–73

electronics, turning off your, 165

embodied decision-making, 147–150

embodying and the intuitive engagement pathway, 202

emotional intelligence, 3, 209

emotional intelligence in business, 27

empathy as a soft skill, 3

employee well-being and organizational success, 208

employees, dealing with problematic, 75–77

enteric brain, the, 136–137

environmental stimuli and the mind, 90

exercise, your perspective and the benefits of, 77

exercising, the conscious mind and, 101

failures, celebrating, 195

fear, inner guidance and, 71–72

fear
     and intuition, 50–54
     in yourself, doubt in the form of, 43–44
     of change, the inner critic and, 117

future behavior, predicting, 7

grandiosity and the inner critic, 115

gross hemispheric specialization, 138

guidance, asking for, 10, 151–169, 215

gut, meetings and listening to your, 137–139

gut
     brain, the, 135–136
     instinct, trusting your, 6–7

intuition, leaders and trusting their, 113

sense and business decisions, 191

head brain, the, 135, 136–137

higher self, guidance from your, 21

hindsight, training intuition and, 94

implicit biases, letting go of, 66

improv classes in business, 198

influence and doubt, 43

information overload, 49

informational intuition, 20, 24–25, 26–31, 158

applying, 209–213

inner compass,
developing the relationship with your, 157–158

doubting your, 44

negotiating and your, 26

the language of your, 30

the source of your, 21

your ego and your, 57

inner critic,
active, 109

befriending your, 105–126

core negative beliefs and the, 115

definition of your, 109–113

doubt and your, 45

formation of the, 114–115

grandiosity and the, 115

making friends with your, 118–125

opposite action step and the, 123–125

positive intention of your, 121–122

separating from your, 10, 214–215

the fear of change and the, 117

your intuitive center and your, 108

inner critic
and body language, the, 119

and confirmation bias, the, 113

and doubt, the, 110

and internalized messaging, the, 114–115

and intuitive intelligence, 110

and parental messaging, the, 114–115

and restoring self-leadership, the, 122–123

and self-leadership, the, 120

and the self, the, 113–114

at work, 115–117

versus intuition, 111–113

inner critic's shape, mapping your, 118–119

inner guidance,
asking questions and, 163–164

fear and, 71–72

importance of listening to, 18

listening proactively to, 29

listening to insecurities and your, 56

self–fulfillment and, 38

inner guidance
and directional intuition, 157

and patience, 164–165

inner guidance system, receiving answers from your, 66–67

inner intelligence,
acting on your, 11, 171–187, 215

overriding your, 176

inner intelligence and doubt, 43

inner knowing, 9

inner navigational system, elements of your, 66

inner sense, following our, 176

inner signals, staying connected to your, 65

inner signals in the sales conversation, 95

inner voice, creating a relationship with your, 37–38

innovation,
encouraging, 196

inner guidance and, 29

innovation and intuition, 6

insecurities and your inner guidance, 56

instinct, gut, 6–7

instinct versus intuition, 30

intelligence, emotional, 3

internalized messaging, the inner critic and, 114–115

interrupting your routine, 72–73

intuitional language, 39

intuitive center and your inner critic, your, 108

intuitive decision-making, leaders and, 192

intuitive engagement pathway, 199–202

intuitive guidance, how to pursue your, 69

intuitive intelligence, 4

    accessing 39

    building our, 160–161

intuitive intelligence
    and company culture, 189

    and the inner critic, 110

intuitive judgments, 4

intuitive language, decoding your, 166–167

intuitive nature, your ego and, 55

intuitive skills, building, 8

intuitive thinking, 8

judgments, intuitive, 4

language, intuitional, 39

leaders and company culture, 190

leadership, adaptive, 142

leadership,
    adaptive, 41, 185–186

    strengthening, 209

leading and the intuitive engagement pathway, 202

left brain versus right brain, 137–138

leisure time, society's view of, 47–48

life experience, the rational mind and, 40

listening and the intuitive engagement pathway, 201

listening proactively to inner guidance, 29

listening skills, improving, 209

listening to your body, 127–150

listening to your gut during meetings, 137–139

long hours, society's view of, 47–48

manipulation and doubt, 43

mapping your inner critic's shape, 118–119

marketing and the power of the subconscious mind, 144–150

meditation
    and doubt, 46

    and improving performance, 89

    in the workplace, 7

mental chatter, 39

mentor, benefits of having a, 157

military strategies and intuition, 28

mind, valuing our conscious rational, 142

mindfulness
    in the workplace, 7

    practices and doubt, 46

    technique, a basic, 102–103

mindfulness-based practices, intuition and, 30–31

mindset, changing your, 88

mindset and strategic thinking, 72

momentum, small decisions and, 181–182

motivation of your inner critic, understanding the, 111–112

navigating conflict, 209

negotiating and your inner compass, 26

negotiation and ego, 57

neural networks throughout the body, 134

neural receptors and the body's cells, 138

nonconscious, tuning into your body and accessing your, 141–144

nonconscious mind,
    accessing your, 39

    activities that free up your, 101

    improving performance and the, 89

nonconscious states, slowing down to access deep, 95

nonverbal communication,
    training, 209

    tracking, 24

obstacles to intuition, five, 33–60

one-on-one sessions, receptivity and, 79

open communication, creating an atmosphere of, 193

opposite action step, the inner critic and, 123–125

organizational success and employee well-being, 208

orientation,
changing your, 88

shifting your, 66

out loud, saying decisions, 166

outside pressures, dealing with, 65

outside-the-box thinking, 40

overconfidence, combating, 4–5

overwhelm, 49

parental messaging and the inner critic, 114–115

patience, inner guidance and, 164–165

pause, the benefits of taking a, 77–80

perception in a reactive state, your, 42

perceptions and reality, 5

personal agenda, intuition and your, 57

personal time, the importance of, 196

perspective,
changing your, 77

learning how to shift your, 72–77

physical activities and dobut, 45

physiological response of fear, 50

positive intention of your inner critic, 121–122

presence, the benefits of, 99–100

pressures, dealing with outside, 65

problem-solving, reactive, 78

problematic employees, dealing with, 75–77

productive, redefining what it means to be, 88–89

psychology and intuition, 3

question, benefits of asking yourself a, 74

questions,
asking powerful, 161–162

responding to, 78–79

quiet time, carving out, 88

rational mind, intuition and the, 38–42

reactive problem-solving, 78

reactive state, your perception in a, 42

reality,
perceptions and, 5

the ego and organizing, 59

receptive,
becoming more, 10, 214

the importance of being, 19

receptivity,
pausing before responding and, 77–78

shifting your center to, 66

shifting your orientation to, 147

receptivity
and business meetings, 79

and one-on-one sessions, 79

in business meetings, 79

reference point, locating your own, 27–28

reflective thinking, carving out time for, 193

relaxation activities, slowing down and, 99–100

resistance, inner guidance and, 71–72

respect, creating an atmosphere of, 193

responding to questions, 78–79

right brain versus left brain, 137–138

risk and safety, 192–195

routine, interrupting your, 72–73

safety and risk, 192–195

sales conversations, inner signals in, 95

sales recordings, slowing down and, 94–95

sales, training intuition in, 92–96

self,
core identity of, 55

the inner critic and the, 113–114

self-authority and intuition, 43

self-awareness as a soft skill, 3

self-concept and ego, 54–59

self-destructive thoughts, the rational mind and, 42

self-doubt, shifting your orientation from, 147

self-fulfillment and inner guidance, 38

self-image and intuition, 54–59

self-leadership,
　　restoring, 122–123

　　the inner critic and, 120

shifting
　　your attention, intuition and, 72

　　your center to receptivity, 66

　　your orientation, 66

silence, the benefits of, 98–99

skills,
　　building intuitive, 8

　　soft, 3

　　technical, 3

slow thinking, intuition and, 88

slowing down,
　　intuition and, 10

　　shifting your orientation to, 147

　　the benefits of, 68–69, 74

　　the importance of, 214

　　the trifecta of, 96–102

slowing down
　　and state changes, 101

　　from your conscious mind stream, 91

　　physically, the benefits of, 73

　　your thinking, benefits of, 88

smartphone dependency, 67

social dynamics in business, 27

social intuition, 20, 22–24, 93, 158

　　applying, 205–209

　　integrating, 26–31

soft skills, 3

space to listen, carving out, 88

speed of thoughts, the, 39

SPT, 64–65

state changes, slowing down and, 101

stillness, the benefits of, 96–98

stillness as an antidote to busyness, 48

strategic thinking, carving out time for, 193

strategic thinking and mindset, 72

strengthening leadership, 209

stressful situations, connecting deeply
　　during, 65

subconscious mind,
　　environmental stimuli and the, 90

　　guidance from your, 21

　　marketing and the power of the, 144–150

subconscious mind,
　　technology and the power of the,
　　144–150

subjective confidence, 4

sustainability, the ego and, 59

synergetic play therapy, see SPT

teaching and the intuitive engagement
　　pathway, 202

technical skills, 3

technology, the inundation of digital, 29

technology and the power of the
　　subconscious mind, 144–150

thoughts,
　　learning to identify and separate
　　your, 42

　　the speed and volume of your, 39

three brains, the, 133–137

training intuition
　　and hindsight, 94

　　in sales, 92–96

trusting and the intuitive engagement
pathway, 201

voice of intuition, discovering the, 37

volume of thoughts, the, 39

vulnerability, leaning into, 162–163

walk, the benefits of taking a, 73

workaholics, society's view of, 47–48

yoga in the workplace, 7

About the Author

Rick Snyder is the founder and CEO of Invisible Edge, an international consulting firm that builds high-performance environments in major, mid-size, and emerging businesses. He leads the Invisible Edge coaches in training companies and teams to build intuitive skills and translate them into business plans and company cultures that result in more effective communication, engagement, profitability, and innovative success. His breakthrough strategies have been implemented by executives and businesses in Europe, Canada, Asia, Africa, and America. Rick holds an MA in psychology and has previously worked in the health-care, tourism and travel, and training spaces. He has launched four businesses and travels extensively between California and Europe for work and leisure, and to help people access their intuitive skills for decision-making on a global scale. For more information on live presentations, trainings, and virtual learning programs for you and your teams, please consult *www.Invisible-EdgeLLC.com*.